Pedro Andrea

PEDRO ANDREA:
The owner of the collection, layout of the dioramas and compiler of the texts
www.pedroandrea.com

SEZAR BLUE:
Photography, editing the layout and texts
sezarblue@terra.es

FINA BAÑO:
Photographic assistant

PEDRO LOZANO:
Photographer 'Caravan Wagon', Sheriff Pasquinades', 'Masked Man', 'Black Moose', 'Red Archer', 'Green Radio', 'Jeep Manoeuvres, Stage One, "Special Patrol', 'Cosmic Link', Illustrations 1 and 8 from the catalogues, boxes (these items are from his own collection) and collaboration with the documentation.
Photo Kenia Safari (Hunter version)
David Cobos Gómez
Editorial manager
JAVIER HUERTA

Published by
ANDREA PRESS
C/ Talleres, 21- Pol. Ind. de Alpedrete
28430 Alpedrete (Madrid)
Tel.: 91 857 00 08 – Fax: 91 857 00 48
www.andrea-miniatures.com
andrea@andrea-miniatures.com

Layout
ANDREA PRESS

Printed by
GRÁFICAS EUROPA

© 2007 Andrea Press
All rights reserved. It is forbidden to totally or partially copy any of the pictures, texts and drawings by printing, photocopying or by any other system without prior written permission of Andrea Press.

ISBN.: 978-84-96658-04-2
Depósito Legal: S. 278-2007

PROLOGUE

To describe Pedro Andrea is simple: a multifaceted man, with a prodigious, overpowering yet amusing mentality. He is deservedly famous due, above all, by virtue of his musical talents. He is a composer of music and writer of lyrics, a virtuoso instrumentalist on both the electric guitar and trumpet, as witnessed by his six solo CDs, and through his work as both a studio and live musician together with Miguel Bosé, Ana Torroja, Cómplices, Luz Casal, Bisbal, Rosana, David Sumers...the list is endless. However, through this book, Pedro introduces us to yet another, totally different passion of his, that of collecting action figures, more specifically those of Madelman.

Pedro Andrea is one of the oldest collectors of Madelman in Spain and it was thanks to our mutual hobby that, in 1991, we met, although, by this time, Pedro had already been collecting figures for some time –if one realises that, by this juncture, he already owned something in the region of seven 'Western Caravans' giving us an idea of the number of items already in his collection. However, Pedro is not only significant because of the scope of his collection, he was also one of the first (together with Yoon Lee) to be interested in, and to systemise in writing (books in English and American) how the hobby was structured. In addition, there is no doubt that he was one of the first to underline the importance to the mass of collectors of original boxes, catalogues, and in the way of assessing the state of 'loose' items, etc. From my own point of view, Pedro was, and is the first purist if we take into account the intention of his collection, the meticulous way he collects, the relationship between individual items, and the fidelity and authenticity of the collection. On this occasion, Pedro presents his 'loose' collection, the unboxed ones and, for many people, the most active and attractive way of collecting because only by holding and touching the figures can they be given a form of 'life'. It is a complete collection, including all the little details, and is an example for all Madelman collectors. Carles Carrera (Professor Quatermass) maintains that, according to the patent dated 22nd February 1968, the number of figures produced will soon be 40 and the book you hold in your hands is, without doubt, a commemoration of this historical event.

Pedro Lozano Crespo
Facultad de Bellas Artes (Fine Arts Faculty)
Universidad Complutense de Madrid
Redaction and photography
of the MADELMAN collectable
(ALTAYA publishing house)

MADELMAN

INTRODUCTION

It was the insolvency of a company devoted to the production of plastic items that initiated the first step in the story of the figure that is the main focus of this book. The name of the company in question was MADEL (Manufacturas Delgado) and during the 1950s it developed a line of toys and household items. Production continued for approximately ten years.

When it finally ceased trading, the Andrés and Arnau families (these latter were the owners of EXIN), purchased the company name in order to continue production of the earlier figures while also planning to introduce new, higher quality ones. Among them was MADELMAN; a new, fully articulated figure that was greeted with such enthusiasm on the market that it soon become the primary product, displacing some others. This fortuitous initiative had as its inspiration GI-JOE (1964-1979), a 30cm figure (1:6 scale) that was articulated by means of an ingenious system of hooks and elastic bands. There were so many fundamental differences with the original MADELMAN (17 cm high, 1:11 scale) the mobility of which was designed around a nylon skeleton, glue and two screws) that it could not be viewed as a mere simple copy. However, in the view of many people, this later MADELMAN was, in fact, just an improved version of the former ones. Still, whatever view held, it cannot be denied that it holds an important position in the history of the articulated figure.

FIRST STAGE

It was for the Christmas of 1968 that the first three MADELMAN models appeared: The Assault Trooper, The Mountain Trooper (a skier in white) and a Sailor. The following year these items, initially sold in individual red boxes, were followed by the Safari Hunter, the Porter and the Spaceman 2001. They were inferior versions of the original as the eyes were hand painted (cornea included) and the wrists were fixed to the forearms so they could not be turned. This same model was also included in the two missions that from 1969 to 1971 were sold by the MADEL company.

The doll with 'crystal eyes' and movable wrists was the most popular figure from 1970 (it coincided with the last year of the missions) until 1976, and it was maybe the most remembered afterwards. This doll, as with its predecessor, had no feet, just rounded ends with a hole to firmly fix the boot. Many of the additions of this brand to the toy industry emerged around this figure while MADEL gained, not only the respect but also the prestige that continues even today. During this period (1970-1976), the company released 26 individual dolls, 13 basic sets, 5 supersets and 7 accessories (all, except the helicopter, were included with other sets besides being sold individually).

The individual dolls were sold with relatively little equipment, although this was increased in some series, for example the 'Basic' sets, the 'Super' sets and the 'Accessory' sets. Others, including the 'Polar Exploration', 'Safari', etc, were sold with lots of accessories and, it should be mentioned, during this period, the military series was the most complete.

However, some other series, such as 'Space Research', 'Grand Prix' and 'Navy' that appeared only in an individual format, had very little in the way of accessories when compared to the other models.

SECOND STAGE

In 1976, MADEL completely overhauled its vision of MADELMAN, launching a new dummy equipped with rubber hair and feet, and substituting the 'crystal eyes' with painted eyes. The plastic used was also improved with the new mixture being both ductile and less brittle. This change was immediately noticeable in the thumbs as, on the earlier models, they were very fragile.

During this second stage, a new series appeared that exceeded the pure military ones not least in equipment. This was the 'Western' series. This new series included women (the first ones had appeared in 1977), new racial types such as American Indians and, of course, the wonderful "covered wagon" that is, without doubt, one of the most charismatic additions to the collection. The 'Space Research' series, until then only represented by the 'Spaceman 2001', was expanded with the addition of 'Cosmic' (1980) and the two exceptional 'M7x' spacecraft. The models in this second stage included 48 individual boxes (taking into account the 7 footballers), 17 basic sets, 8 supersets and some accessories that could be included in both periods given their similar characteristics. The cannon, the yellow and green helicopters, the motorboat and the submarine scooter are good examples of this. However, others, such as the sleigh were equipped with a new frame and came in a new colour and a different texture and the original rubber dog was replaced with a plastic one; the Jeep's hard plastic seats were replaced with ones made of material while the trailer, which initially appeared only in the 'Safari' series (a new one for the 'Military' series was launched during this second stage) was improved with the incorporation of a tarpaulin.

The two 'Cosmic' spacecrafts, the 'Tepee', the two horses,

INTRODUCTION

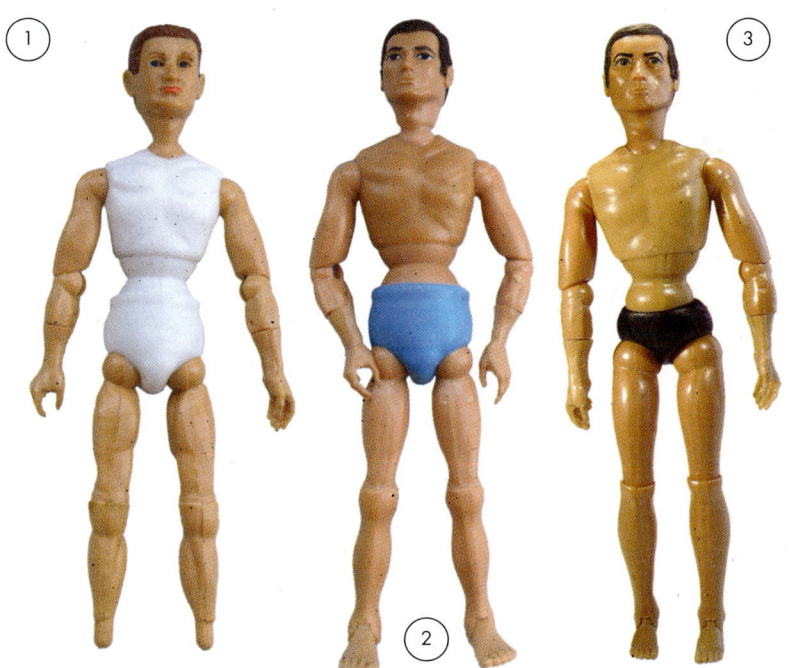

1. First stage Madelman. This doll was manufactured, with some variations, from 1968 to 1975.

2. Second stage Madelman. This dummy was manufactured from 1976 to 1982. It was constructed from shockproof polystyrene for the body with nylon for the internal structure. There was a third version made up from the torso of a male figure combined with the legs of a female figure, as in the cases of 'Superman' and the 'Green Man'.

3. Hybrid dummy 1980-1982, it combined a male trunk with female legs and hips.

the '7th Cavalry' machine Gun, the 'Canoe', the three 'Buggies' and the fortified position were exclusive to this period.

Although MADEL closed its doors in 1983, it continued to launch new models until 1982. During this time, it created the 7 footballers, the 'Red Archer', the 'Masked Man', the 'Black Moose', the 'Canada' superset and the 'Polar Station' before the definitive demise of a company that so many children owed so many hours of enjoyment and so many adults today owe so many hours of nostalgia. Some of these adults, myself included, have had the added bonus, through a mutual collecting pastime, of being able to rekindle a friendship with a playmate of long ago. Together we are part of an innumerable band of collectors who have created a market that has seen some pieces reach record prices. For example, the 'Safari Mission' has changed hands for as much as 4900 euros while the 'Flag of Campaign Mission' has gone for as much as 240 euros. In addition, Madelman figures have spawned many exhibitions, conventions and even been the subject of a number of initiatives oriented towards the copying of the various figures. All these activities go some way to underlining the fact that the company, and its product, has left an indelible impression on many people.

It goes without saying that this book is just one of the many consequences of this growing hobby. Its aim is to illustrate the collection in a complete and accurate way and to be used as a reference tool for anyone interested in the subject.

On the other hand, it is also an attempt to clearly illustrate the spontaneity of movement and natural positions that each figure offers (all thanks to the unique design by modelers such as Vicnete Puig or Jaume Vila among others). It is these qualities that make the figures so unique among others of their generation and the reason behind the decision to display the collection out of their boxes.

It is interesting to note that throughout the Madelman production many contradictions appeared between those models displayed in the catalogue and the ones that finally appeared on the market. One clear example is the 'Hook Pirate' that was released during the first stage: the catalogue showed a figure sporting white and red striped trousers and a blue shirt, while the figure that appeared on the market wore grey trousers and a white and brown striped shirt. The items displayed in this book are the most exact approximation to the number and variation of pieces offered in the most frequent versions of each item. Given the internal policies of MADEL, it is inevitable that there exists a number of different versions, as pertains to the colours and equipment, to the ones shown here.

Finally, it must be pointed out that the 'Safari' and 'Pirates' dioramas have been displayed to include all its figures, accessories and fittings from both the first and second stages. On the other hand, the 'Military' and 'Western' dioramas do not include all their accessories as there are too many and, to include them, the resultant photographs would be so small that it would be near impossible to fully appreciate all the details.

MADELMAN

FIRST STAGE
Red boxes

The three models presented here were launched during Christmas 1968 and were displayed in individual red boxes.

(1968/1970)

Equipment	SAILOR
2 Signal flags	1 Signal gun

There were some copies carrying binoculars. Compare this with its second version on Page 60.

(1968/1970)

Equipment	ASSAULT TROOPS
1 Thompson machine gun	1 Helmet

Equipment	MOUNTAIN TROOPS	
1 Cap	2 Ski poles	
2 Skis	1 Binoculars	

(1968/1970)

FIRST STAGE

The three models shown here were launched in 1969, and were the last to be displayed in the individual red box format.

Regarding the Madelman 'Porter', it should be pointed out that this figure's skeleton from 1968-1970, was made from black nylon. This can be easily seen on the front of the elbows and behind the knees.

Equipment	2001 SPACEMAN
1 Helmet	1 Knapsack (chest and backpack)

1968 / 1970

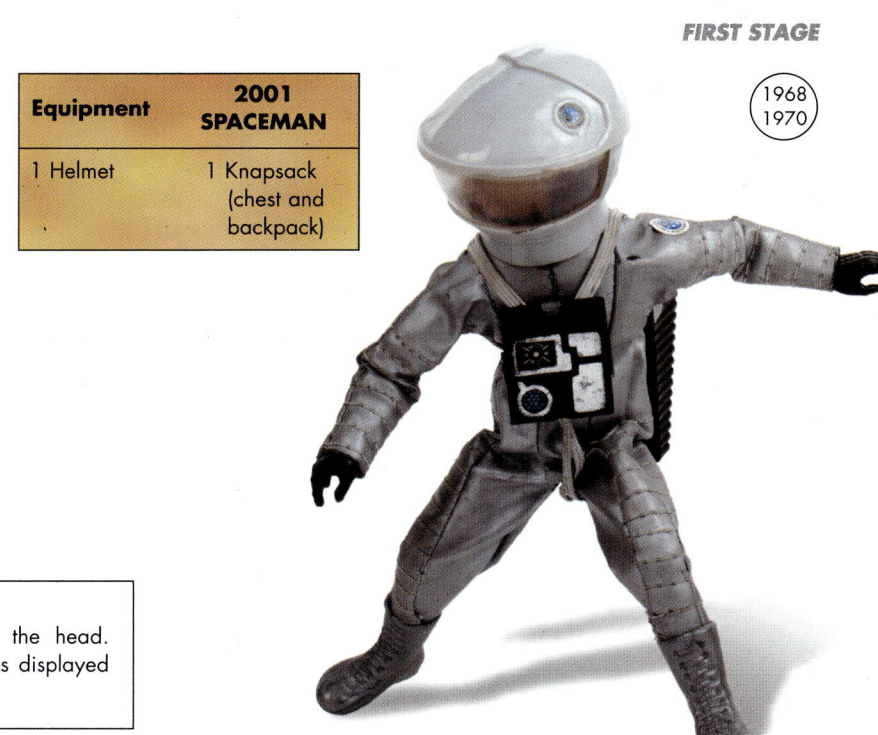

Equipment	SAFARI HUNTER
1 Water bottle	
1 Rifle	
1 Colt (black)	
1 Monkey	
1 Salacot [1]	

(1) Salacot
It was stuck on the head. From 1970 it was displayed separately.

1969 / 1970

Equipment	PORTER	
1 Colt (black)	1 Machete	
1 Monkey	1 Fez [1]	

(1) Fez
Throughout its production it was stuck on the head. ≠

1969 / 1970

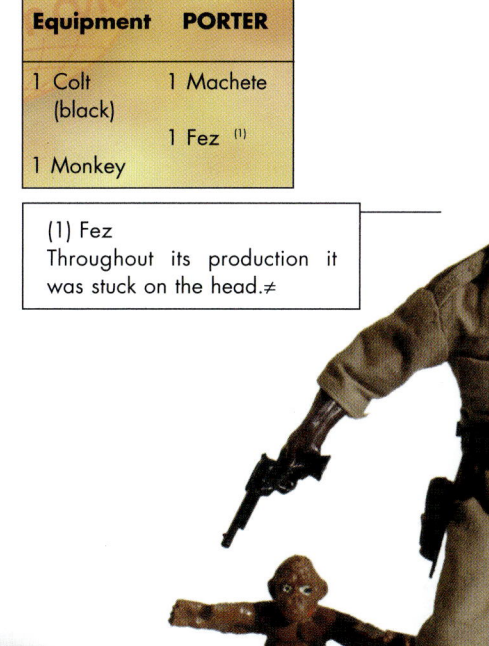

This diorama shows all the figures, fittings and accessories offered by MADEL in individual equipment sets, basic sets, super-sets and safari mission in both stages of the series.

MADELMAN

Individual sets

Equipment	MOUNTAIN TROOPS MOUNTAINEER
1 Water bottle	1 Cap
1 Rifle	1 Rope

1971 / 1975

The following models had 'crystal' eyes and movable wrists that could be rotated and retained the fixing system instead of feet as with the former models. These new models were launched in a much more colourful format and the box sizes were larger than the original red ones.

1971 / 1975

1971 / 1975

Equipment	PORTER
1 Fez	
1 Bundle of cloth	
4 Elephant tusks	
1 Machete	
1 Colt (black)	

Equipment	SAFARI HUNTER
1 Salacot	1 Water bottle
1 Monkey	1 Colt (black)
1 Rifle	

10

FIRST STAGE

1971 / 1975

Equipment	MOUNTAIN TROOPS SAPPER
1 Cap	1 Spade
1 Ice axe	1 Knapsack (1)

(1) Knapsack
This contained a green blanket.

Equipment	POLAR EXPEDITION SNOWSHOES
2 White snowshoes	1 Ski poles
	1 Binoculars

1971 / 1975

1971 / 1975

Equipment	SPELEOLOGIST
1 Helmet	1 Rope
1 Ice axe	1 Gas lamp (orange)

1971 / 1975

Equipment	POLAR EXPEDITION SKIS
2 Skis	1 Rifle
2 Ski poles	

MADELMAN

Equipment	POLAR EXPEDITION TROOP
2 White skis	1 Cap
2 Ski poles	1 Rifle

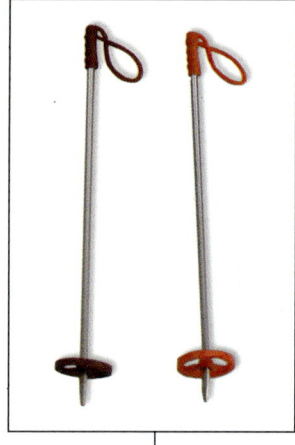

(1971 / 1975)

In the first version the ski poles were paler than in the second version.

(1971 / 1975)

Equipment	SCUBA DIVER RECONNAISSANCE
1 Knife with scabbard	1 Snorkel
1 Goggles	1 Harpoon [1]

(1) Harpoon
The frame was made of plastic with a metal shaft.

Equipment	SCUBA DIVER DEMOLITION
1 Goggles	1 Watch
3 Dynamite charges	1 Mine

(1971 / 1975)

12

FIRST STAGE

Equipment	NAVY MARINE
1 Helmet	
1 Machine gun	
1 Radio transmitter	
1 Gun (1)	
1 Binoculars (2)	

1973 1975

(1) Gun
The belt was identical to that in the 'Anti-tank' and 'Military Police' sets, and had a hook originally used for the policeman's truncheon.

(2) Binoculars
The majority of the versions were not equipped with binoculars although some models, as with this one, included it.

In 1972 and 1973, the sailor was launched in two different versions. Shown here are both versions with all their respective equipment (first stage).

1972 1975

1971 1975

Equipment	NAVY SAILOR	
	In 1972	**In 1973**
	1. Kitbag with number N-2371	1. Kitbag with number N-2371
	1 Anchor	1 Blue briefcase containing a 'Naval Invasion Tactic' map

Equipment	NAVY AIRCRAFT CARRIER	
1 Binoculars		2 Signal flags
1 Helmet		
		1 Life jacket

MADELMAN

Equipment	ARMY RADIO OPERATOR
1 Helmet	1 Radio with earphones

1970 / 1975

1971 / 1975

Equipment	ARMY COMMANDO
1 Helmet	
1 Machine gun	
1 Silver radio transmitter	
6 Hand grenade	

1972 / 1975

Equipment	ARMY MILITARY POLICE
1 Helmet	1 Truncheon
1 Gun	1 Silver radio transmitter

14

FIRST STAGE

(1971 / 1975)

Equipment	ARMY MEDIC
1 Helmet (with Red Cross sticker)	1 Bandage roll
	1 White box with a Red Cross on the top
1 Medical bag containing 4 medicine containers	1 Transparent bottle
	1 White bottle

(1970 / 1975)

Equipment	ARMY ASSAULT TROOPS
1 Helmet	1 Thompson machine gun
1 Sandbag	

MADELMAN

(1974 / 1975)

Equipment	GRAND PRIX BOXES
1 Cap	1 Ferrari sticker on the left side of chest with another on the back
1 Blackboard	
1 Pencil (1)	
1 Tool boxes (2)	

(1) Pencil
On one side is the inscription 'Lapiz-hito'.

(2) Tool box
fixed with Sellotape, the box contained the following tools:

1 screwdriver	1 hammer
1 spanner	1 adjustable spanner
1 pneumatic drill	1 pliers

(1974 / 1975)

Equipment	GRAND PRIX TEST DRIVER
1 Helmet (1)	1 Trophy
1 Circuit diàgram	

(1) Helmet
Usually red, although the first version was white.

Three stickers stood out with this model: a Texaco one on the helmet and two on the jacket, one of the Spanish flag and the other of Alfa Romeo. There were additional stickers on each trouser leg and a further, yellow one, on the helmet.

FIRST STAGE

Equipment	SPACE RESEARCH 2001 SPACEMAN
1 Helmet [1]	1 Knapsack (1 chestpack, 1 backpack)
1 Sticker on the left shoulder [2]	

(1) Helmet
This had 3 stickers, two on the top with 'United States Astronautics Discovery' and another on the rear depicting a module panel.

(2) Sticker
This was identical to the above but larger.

1972 1975

1974 1975

1974 1975

Equipment	CANADA MOUNTED POLICE (RCMP)
1 Hat	
1 Radio transmitter	
1 Gun with safety catch	

Equipment	CANADA HUNTER
1 Rubber cap	1 Rifle
1 Knife	1 Powder horn

17

MADELMAN

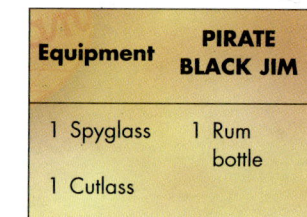

Equipment	PIRATE BLACK JIM
1 Spyglass	1 Rum bottle
1 Cutlass	

1975

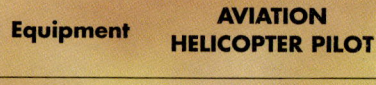

Equipment	AVIATION HELICOPTER PILOT
1 Cap	1 Briefcase with a plan (battle lines)
1 Radio transmitter	

1974 1975

1975

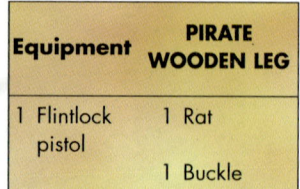

Equipment	PIRATE WOODEN LEG
1 Flintlock pistol	1 Rat
	1 Buckle

18

Basic equipment

The Basic Equipment sets were launched in larger boxes than the individual ones as they offered more accessories.

Equipment	MOUNTAIN TROOPS
1 Cap	1 Water bottle
1 Knapsack [1]	1 Mortar
1 Rope	8 Rounds for the mortar
1 Ice axe	1 Box with opening lid
1 Spade	1 Silver radio transmitter
1 Signal gun	

FIRST STAGE

(1970 1975)

(1) Knapsack
This contained a green blanket.

MADELMAN

Equipment	MECHANIC SERVICE STATION
1 Petrol pump	1 Jack
1 Tool box [1]	1 Petrol can
1 Oil tin	

(1) Tool box contained the same tools as in the mechanic's box:

1 screwdriver	1 hammer
1 spanner	1 adjustable spanner
1 pneumatic drill	1 pliers

1970 / 1975

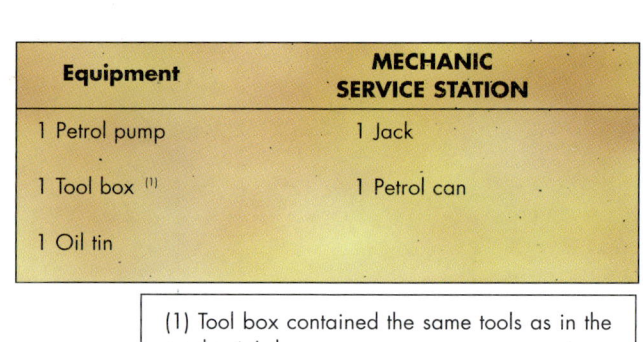

Equipment	SCUBA DIVER
1 Rubber raft with anchor and paddle	
1 Harpoon (plastic frame and metal shaft)	
1 Flashlight	
1 Knife and scabbard	
1 Oxygen bottle	
1 Goggles	
3 Dynamite charges	
1 Watch	

1970 / 1975

Detail of the watch.

20

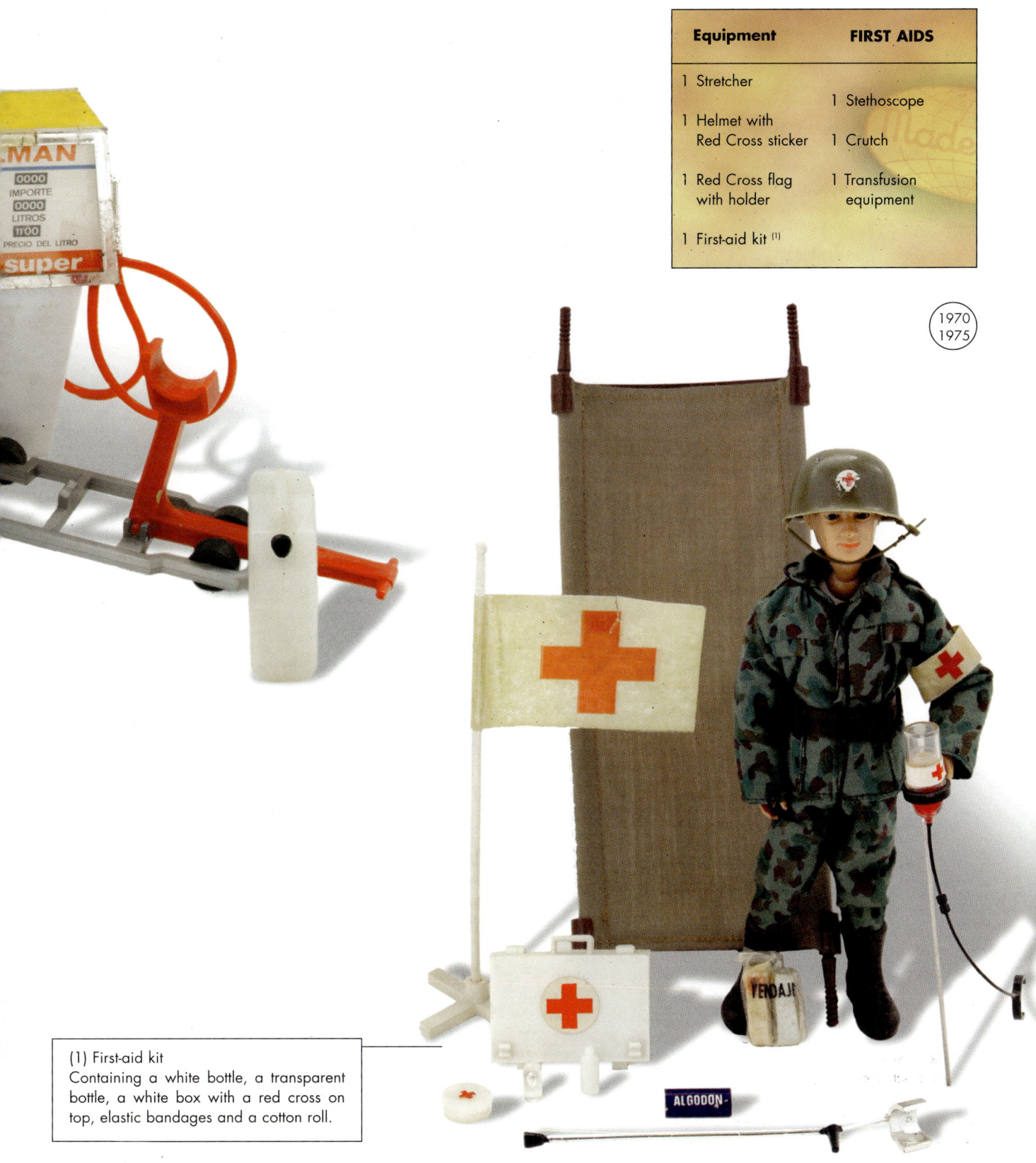

FIRST STAGE

Equipment	FIRST AIDS
1 Stretcher	1 Stethoscope
1 Helmet with Red Cross sticker	1 Crutch
1 Red Cross flag with holder	1 Transfusion equipment
1 First-aid kit [1]	

1970 1975

(1) First-aid kit
Containing a white bottle, a transparent bottle, a white box with a red cross on top, elastic bandages and a cotton roll.

MADELMAN

Equipment	SPELEOLOGIST
1 Helmet	1 Spade
	1 Rope ladder
1 Ice axe	
	1 Winch
1 Flashlight (orange)	
	1 Water bottle

1970 / 1975

Equipment	POLAR EXPEDITION
1 Sleigh	2 White snowshoes
1 Rubber dog with protective covering	1 Whip
1 Cooker	1 Blanket

1970 / 1975

22

FIRST STAGE

(1971–1975)

Equipment	HUNTER
1 Rubber cap	1 Knife
1 Rifle	1 Operable hunting trap
1 Rustic sleigh	1 Gunpowder horn
1 Haversack	1 Fox

This composition shows the high number of possibilities offered by the articulation of Madelman figures to allow them to attain the most dynamic positions.

MADELMAN

Map detail.

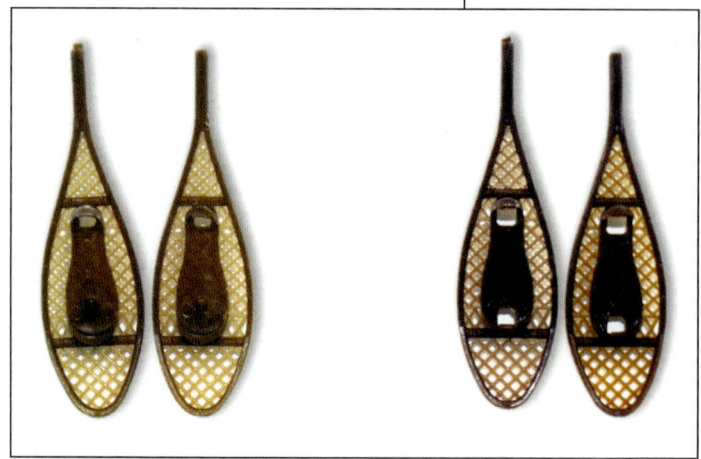

○ 1971 1975

(1) Briefcase.
It contains a map with geographical positions, tribes and animals.

(2) Snowshoes.
Compare the First Stage ones on the left with those from the Second Stage on the right.

Equipment	CANADIAN MOUNTED POLICE
1 Cap	1 Pistol
1 Briefcase (1)	1 Dog
2 Brown snowshoes (2)	1 Rifle
1 Radio transmitter	1 Binoculars

FIRST STAGE

Equipment	SCUBA DIVER
1 Diving suit with bib	1 Knife and scabbard
1 Snorkel	1 Pair of clogs [3]
1 Scapular [1]	1 Buoy with position flag
1 Chest [2]	1 Air pump [4]

(1) Scapular.
Two plastic pieces on the chest and back to act as ballast.

1973 1975

(2) Chest.
This contains a template for simulating gold coins and a bag with jewels of different shapes and colours.

(3) Pair of clogs.
The soles were two weights to enable the figure to be submerged.

(4) Air pump.
This item could be connected to a rubber pump that supplied air so that the figure could submerge when this device was connected to the diving suit.

MADELMAN

Equipment	ANTITANK
1 Helmet	1 Box containing three bazooka rounds
1 Pistol [1]	
1 Flamethrower	1 Transparent plastic bag containing six hand grenades
1 Bazooka [2]	

(1974 / 1975)

(1) Pistol.
The holster was identical to the one supplied with the 'Marine' and 'Military Police' sets.

(2) Bazooka.
It could fire projectiles by means of a spring.

(1975)

Equipment	SAFARI GUIDE
1 Hat	1 Rifle
1 Chimpanzee	1 Black Panther
1 Colt (black)	1 Hunting net [1]
1 Water canteen	1 Map (Kenya safari)

(1) Hunting net.
This was more transparent than the one supplied with the second version.

FIRST STAGE

1974
1975

Equipment	GUERRILLA SOLDIER
1 Hat	3 Dynamite charges
1 Binoculars	1 Mortar [1]
1 Pistol	1 Transparent plastic bag containing six hand grenades
1 Detonator	
1 Reel with cable of black thread	1 Hook
	1 Radio transmitter [2]

(1) Mortar.
It could launch both projectiles and the hook by means of an internal spring and was identical to that supplied with the 'Mountain Trooper' set.

(2) Radio transmitter.
This model, unlike the silver one, had a needle as a retractable antenna.

MADELMAN

Equipment   PIRATE
1 Pirate flag and stand
1 Sword
1 Flintlock pistol
1 Cabin lantern
1 Spyglass
1 Chest [1]
1 Treasure map
1 Rum cask
3 Rats

(1974 / 1975)

[1] Chest.
This contained a template for simulating gold coins and a bag with jewels of different shapes and colours.

The super equipment series

This chapter introduces the five 'Super Equipment' sets that were released during the first stage. Each one included two Madelman, a large number of accessories along with other accessories that were also sold separately, such as the scooter (Submarine Research) or the sleigh (Polar Station). As can be imagined, these were the largest sets, along with the 'Mission' sets that will be examined later.

FIRST STAGE

Equipment	KENYA SAFARI HUNTER AND PORTER	
1 Black Panther [1]	1 Map	1 Gas lantern (blue)
1 Tent [2]	1 White radio, with black front panel and earphones	4 Elephant tusks
2 Monkeys		
1 White cloth bag containing four medicine containers	2 Black Colts	1 Six-walled cage
	1 Table and two chairs	1 Rifle
1 Machete		

(1) Black Panther.
There was a second version containing a lion instead of a panther.

1975

Detail of the map.

(2) Tent.
It consisted of five poles, soil and canvas.

MADELMAN

POLAR STATION (2 MADELMAN)

Equipment		
2 Pairs of white snowshoes	1 Anemometer, rainmeter and tripod	1 Penguin
1 Sleigh and dog	1 Cooker	1 Radio and earphones [2]
1 Whip	1 Fish, reel and fishing line	
1 Plastic base [1]		

(1) Plastic surface. It simulated a hollow in the ice. The water was simulated by means of a cardboard sheet.

(2) Radio. In grey with a black front panel.

1971 1975

FIRST STAGE

(1) Tent.
This tent was identical to the one supplied with the 'Safari Super Equipment' set and consisted of five poles and canvas.

1974 1975

Equipment	HIGH COMMAND OFFICER AND SOLDIER
1 Tent [1]	1 Gas lantern (blue)
2 Ammunition boxes	1 Bazooka and four projectiles
1 Table and chair	1 Operable mortar
3 Sandbags	6 Hand grenades in a transparent plastic bag
1 Pistol	
1 Machine gun	1 Radio transmitter
1 Briefcase and map (High Command Attack)	1 Binoculars
	1 Green field radio and earphones

MADELMAN

Equipment	SUBMARINE RESEARCH (2 SCUBA DIVERS)
2 Amphorae [1]	1 Chest, identical to the one supplied with the basic equipment
1 Submarine scooter	
2 Oxygen cylinders	2 Knifes and scabbards
1 Harpoon made of plastic and metal	1 Watch
	2 Sea horses
2 Diving goggles	1 Octopus [2]
3 Stars with different shapes	1 Flashlight

(1971 1975)

[1] Amphorae.
One broken into two pieces.

[2] Octopus.
Each tentacle has a wire running through it so it can be articulated.

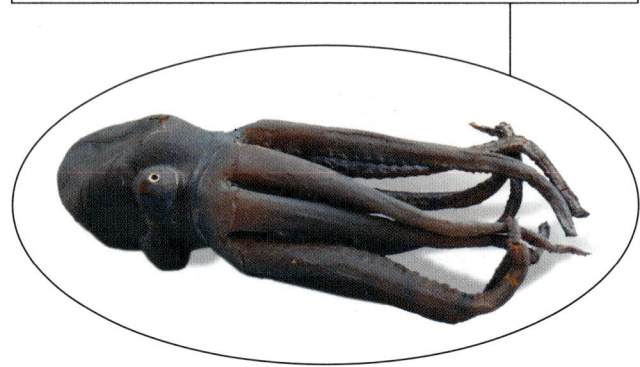

FIRST STAGE

(1) Raft.
With a pole and flag and one paddle acting as a rudder.

Equipment	PIRATE CAPTAIN WOODEN LEG PIRATE AND CAPTAIN		
1 Raft [1]	1 Bottle of rum	1 Axe
1 Chest [2]	1 Cask of rum	1 Retractable spyglass
1 Boathook	1 Powder keg	1 Treasure map
1 Spade	1 Parrot	
1 Cabin lantern	1 Bucket	1 Bicorn
1 Knife	1 Cutlass	1 Ball and chain

1974 1975

(2) Chest.
Identical to the one supplied with the 'Submarine Research' set.

FIRST STAGE

Complements

These were sets released under the title 'COMPLEMENTOS' (Accessories) and were sold separately in closed boxes with an illustration of the contents on the cover. The sets containing figures were supplied in boxes with a transparent cover allowing the contents to be viewed.

GREEN HELICOPTER (1975/1976)

This, like the other Madelman helicopters, had revolving rotors activated by a trigger. The only accessories were a couple of green jerry cans.

CANNON (1974/1980)

This item was first supplied with the 'Mission Campaign' set but was later sold separately.

37

MADELMAN

JEEP SAFARI	
1 Spare wheel	1 White jerry can

SAFARI TRAILER

This trailer was never released as a separate accessory. It was only supplied with the 'Mission Safari' set.

1973 / 1975

JEEP CAMPAIGN	
1 Spare wheel	1 Green jerry can

1973 / 1975

FIRST STAGE

SCOOTER

(1974 1980)

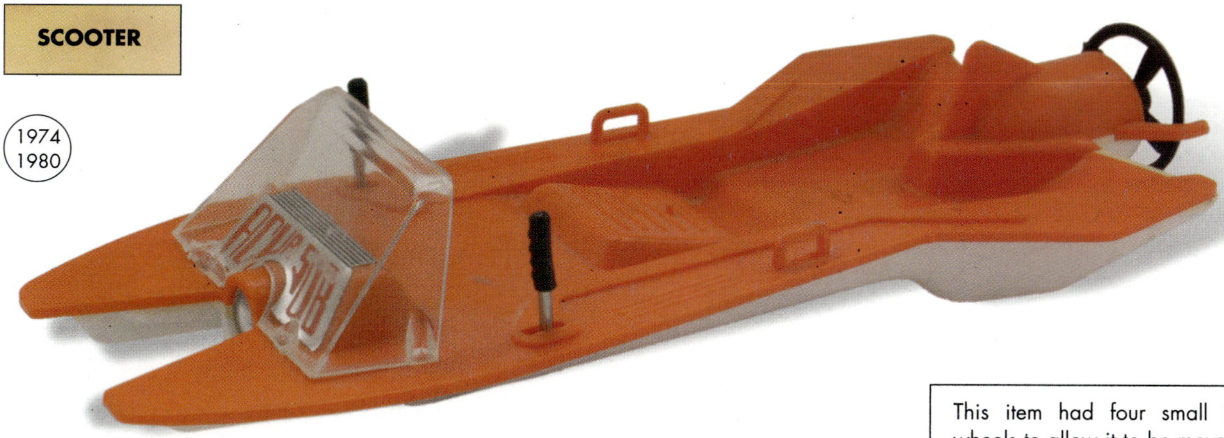

This item had four small interior wheels to allow it to be moved.

LAUNCH

1 Paddle [(1)]   1 Anchor

(1) Paddle. The first versions had only the edge of the paddle painted yellow.

(1974 1980)

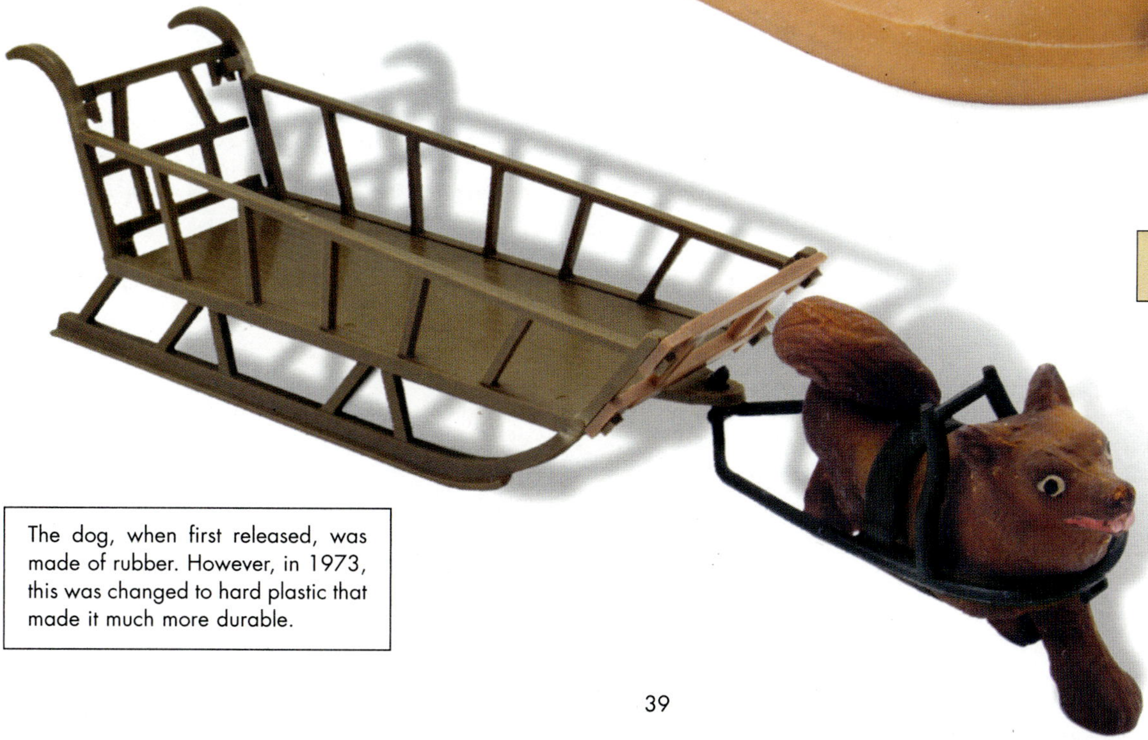

SLEIGH

(1973 1975)

The dog, when first released, was made of rubber. However, in 1973, this was changed to hard plastic that made it much more durable.

39

MADELMAN

Accessories

(1975)

Shown here are the 14 accessory sets that were presented in the 1974-75 catalogue. These sets were the smallest ever produced by MADELMAN. There is also a diagram of one of these sets and the only exclusive item included in this series: the emerald green radio.

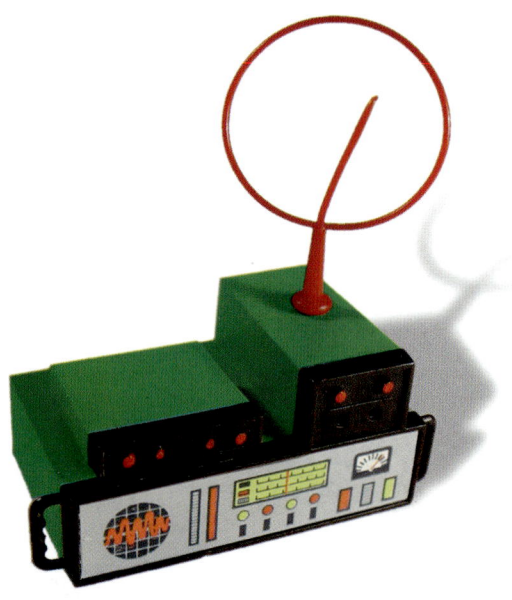

Escalador
Ref. 2.000

Zapador
Ref. 2.001

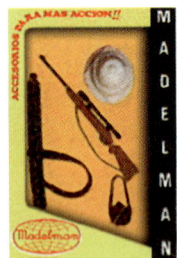
Cazador
Ref. 2.010

Porteador
Ref. 2.011

Safari
Ref. 2.012

Espeleólogo
Ref. 2.020

Raquetas
Ref. 2.031

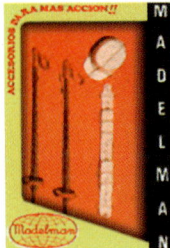
Tropa Expedición Polar
Ref. 2.032

Reconocimiento
Ref. 2.040

Demolición
Ref. 2.041

Campaña
Ref. 2.060

Transmisiones
Ref. 2.061

Tropa de Choque
Ref. 2.064

Socorrismo Campaña
Ref. 2.065

MADELMAN

Mission sets

Shown here are the two 'Mission' sets that were marketed from 1969 to 1971. They were released in opaque boxes. Illustrations by Rafael Cortiella showed what each box contained.

Equipment	SAFARI MISSION (HUNTER AND PORTER)	
	THE SAME MODELS AS SUPPLIED IN THE RED BOX	
2 Colts (black)	3 Monkeys	1 Tent [3]
1 Rifle [1]	2 White jerry cans	1 Table [4] and 2 chairs
1 Water canteen	2 Bales	
1 Cage [2]	1 Orange gas lantern	1 White Jeep and trailer [5]
1 Machete		

1969 1971

FIRST STAGE

(1) Rifle.
This is the one manufactured in the darkest colour: a greyish brown, almost black.

(2) Cage.
With four sides and a roof and soil in injected plastic simulating wood. This item was exclusive to the 'Safari Mission' set.

(3) Tent.
The version shown here is the one usually supplied in this format, although there was another version —displayed in the 'Safari Diorama'- in green. This version is extremely rare and we know of only this example. The soil was black for both 'Mission' sets.

(4) Table.
The yellow table was exclusive to this set.

(5) White Jeep and trailer.
These items were exclusive to this 'Mission' set. The jeep had no stickers and there were no holes in the trailer for fixing the tarpaulin.

MADELMAN

Equipment	CAMPAIGN MISSION (3 MADELMAN) 'RED BOX' MODEL - ASSAULT TROOPS
2 Thompson machine guns	2 Green and one white jerry cans
12 Sandbags	18 Artillery shells and 8 hand grenades
1 White and blue flag plus stand [1]	1 Tent [3]
1 Watch	1 Jeep [4]
2 Boxes [2]	1 Cannon [5]

1969 1971

(1) Flag.
Exclusive to this set.

(2) Boxes.
Each was made of simulated wood and had an opening lid.

(3) Tent.
With 5 poles, canvas and black soil.

(4) Jeep.
With no stickers, an exclusive item.

(5) Cannon.
Without stickers.

FIRST STAGE

# AN ATHEOLOGY

AN ATHEOLOGY

AN ATHEOLOGY

AN ATHEOLOGY

AN ATHEOLOGY

AN ATHEOLOGY

AN ATHEOLOGY

AN ATHEOLOGY

AN ATHEOLOGY

AN ATHEOLOGY

AN ATHEOLOGY

AN ATHEOLOGY

AN ATHEOLOGY

AN ATHEOLOGY

AN ATHEOLOGY

AN ATHEOLOGY

AN ATHEOLOGY

AN ATHEOLOGY

AN ATHEOLOGY

AN ATHEOLOGY

AN ATHEOLOGY

AN ATHEOLOGY

AN ATHEOLOGY

AN ATHEOLOGY

AN ATHEOLOGY

AN ATHEOLOGY

AN ATHEOLOGY

AN ATHEOLOGY

AN ATHEOLOGY

AN ATHEOLOGY

AN ATHEOLOGY

MADELMAN

CATALOGUES AND POSTERS
Catalogues

Shown here is the complete range of MADELMAN catalogues. They were all printed in colour. The 'First Stage' catalogue showed the figures in their boxes, but the 'Second Stage' catalogue showed them out of the boxes. In addition, there was a page showing the boxes of the different series.

The catalogues for the years 1972-73 and 1974-76 had identical covers although new releases were added to each edition. The 1982 catalogue had the same cover as that of the previous year, but the catalogue itself was of a smaller dimension.

1970

1971

1972
1973

1976

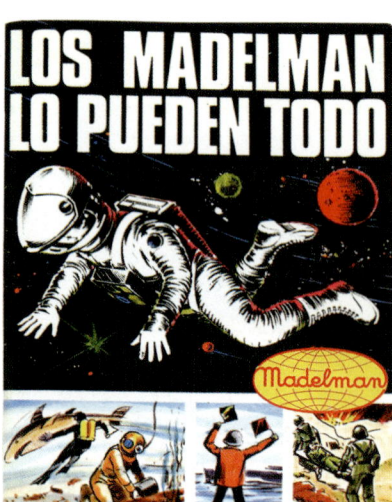
1974
1976

1977

46

CATALOGUES AND POSTERS

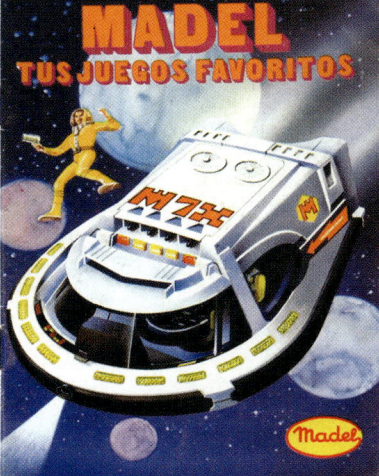
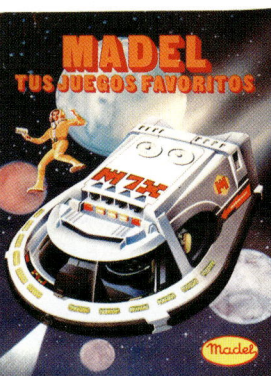

Posters

These posters were released from 1974 and were included with some of the 'Super Equipment' sets. Each measured 48 x 49 cm. The most sought after, almost impossible to find, and, therefore, most valuable, was the one featuring the scuba diver.

| Pirate Captain | Canadian Mounted Police | Hunter | Scuba Diver |

BOXES
First stage

These boxes were released at the end of 1969 and replaced the original red boxes. They were designed for dry assembly without recourse to glue.

Basic equipment box

Two examples of the red boxes from the years 1968 and 1969. The 'Astronaut' box was the only one with one blue face.

BOXES

The boxes were manufactured from grey cardboard coloured on one face. After filling, they were covered in a transparent plastic cover so that the contents could be viewed. When the modern dummy was first released in 1976 (supplied in a different box) the old boxes continued to be used until the old stock was exhausted.

There were a number of boxes featuring a special design. These included the Astronaut 2001 box that was also printed in a different colour. This particular box is highly sought-after by both toy and merchandising collectors as it contained the only dummy ever made that was related to this movie. The content was fixed to the bottom of the box by elastic bands.

Individual box

Super equipment

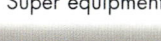

MADELMAN
Second Stage

The individual boxes were punched with flaps. For both the 'Basic' and the 'Super Equipment' sets, the assembly system was similar to that of a matchbox, (as it was commonly known in the factory). The illustrations on the 'First Stage' boxes were done in gouache while for the 'Second Stage' boxes they were done using pantone fibre-tip pens.

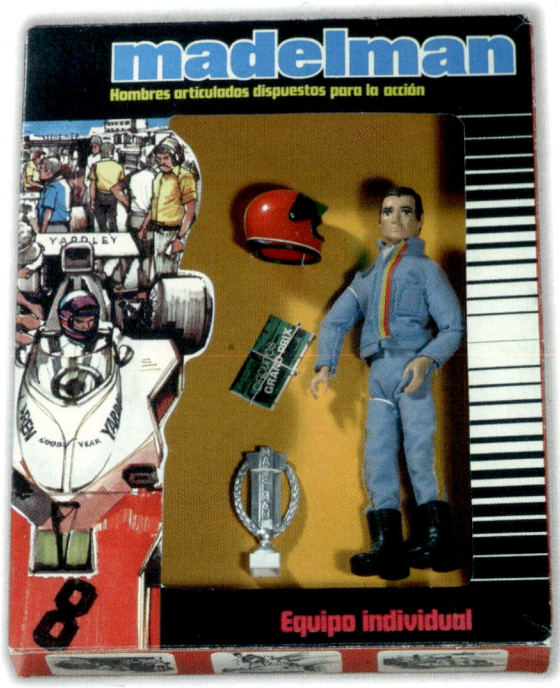

Individual equipment box

Basic equipment box

BOXES

Double equipment box

Super equipment

MADELMAN

SECOND STAGE
Individual sets

A new dummy was manufactured between 1976 and 1982. The most significant differences were painted eyes, rubber hair, the use of a more ductile plastic and the inclusion of feet. The feet could only be articulated up and down with no lateral movement. The former dummy had no feet and the primitive system used allowed the boots to move from side to side.

Equipment	SAFARI HUNTER
1 Salacot [1]	1 Water canteen
1 Rifle	
1 Silver Colt	1 Monkey

1976 1983

(1) Salacot.
Note the differences compared to the 'First Stage' as shown on Page 7.

Equipment	SAFARI EXPLORER
1 Hat [1]	1 Silver Colt
1 Machete	1 Water canteen
1 Rifle	

(1) Hat.
Manufactured in rubber in the 'Second Stage' as opposed to felt in the 'First Stage'.

1980 1983

Equipment	SAFARI PORTER
1 Fez glued to the head	
1 Bale	
1 Machete	
1 Silver Colt	
4 Elephant tusks	

1976 1979

SECOND STAGE

Equipment	SPELEOLOGY SPELEOLOGIST
1 Helmet	1 Ice axe
1 Rope	1 Orange gas lantern

Shown here are the two 'Speleology' sets released in 1982, although the one on the left was initially named 'Face Worker'.

Equipment	POLAR EXPEDITION SKIS
1 Rifle	2 Brown skis
2 Ski poles	

This version had brown fur around the edges of the coat. As can be seen, this differs from other models that had white fur.

1976 1979

Equipment	POLAR EXPEDITION SNOWSHOES
1 Binoculars	2 Snowshoes
1 Ski pole	

53

MADELMAN

1980 1983

Equipment	MOUNTAIN TROOPER SAPPER
1 Peaked cap	
1 Spade	
1 Ice axe	
1 Knapsack [1]	

1976 1977

Detail of the sapper's ice axes. Compare the ice axe on the right, from the 'Second Stage', with the one on the left, from the 'First Stage'.

Equipment	POLAR EXPEDITION METEOROLOGIST
1 Anemometer and tripod	

Note the difference in the colour of the fur around the coat edges.

[1] Knapsack. This contained a green blanket.

1) Peaked cap. This was manufactured from hard rubber instead of the original injected plastic.

(2) Skis. In the 'Second Stage', the skis were fixed to the dummy's feet by means of a pressure system thus abandoning the original system that consisted of a spigot that fitted into a hole in the sole of the boot.

Equipment	POLAR EXPEDITION TROOPER	
1 Peaked cap [1]	2 Skis [2]	
1 Machine gun	2 Ski poles	

1976 1983

SECOND STAGE

1976 1977

Equipment	MOUNTAIN TROOP CLIMBER
1 Peaked cap	1 Rope
1 Rifle	1 Water canteen

Between 1980 and 1983, the 'Climber' and the 'Trooper' were omitted from the catalogue and replaced with a new model: the 'Mountaineer'. This was, in fact, exactly the same set and the accessories consisted of a peaked cap, rope, knapsack and ice axe.

(1) Harpoon.
The plastic frame was retained for the second stage although the original metal shaft was replaced with a plastic one.

Equipment	SCUBA DIVER DEMOLITION
1 Mine [1]	1 Watch
3 Dynamite charges	1 Goggles

1976 1979

1976 1983

Equipment	SCUBA DIVER RECONNAISSANCE
1 Goggles	1 Snorkel
1 Harpoon [1]	1 Knife and scabbard

Please note that this set is purposely displayed in its original box as it is a real antique and the rubber would be in danger of cracking if the dummy was removed from its box and handled.

(1) Mine
Although the mines manufactured during the 'Second Stage' were a darker shade of gray than the one displayed here, they can also be found in a lighter shade since the original 'First Stage' stock continued to be used until exhausted.

MADELMAN

1976 / 1983

Equipment CANADA - HUNTER
- 1 Hat made of rubber
- 1 Powder horn
- 1 Knife
- 1 Haversack
- 1 Rifle

(1) Hat.
This was a felt one identical to the one in the 'First Stage' with some small modifications to fit the dummy's head.

Equipment CANADIAN MOUNTED POLICE
- 1 Hat (1)
- 1 Radio transmitter
- 1 Winchester rifle
- 1 Pistol and safety catch

1976 / 1983

1980 / 1983

Equipment PIRATES DICK THE ONE-EYED PIRATE
- 1 Bicorn
- 1 Spyglass
- 1 Treasure map
- 1 Cutlass

1976 / 1983

Equipment SPACE RESEARCH ASTRONAUT 2001
- 1 Helmet
- 1 Chestpack and backpack

This model had the same stickers as its predecessor.

58

SECOND STAGE

(1976 1983)

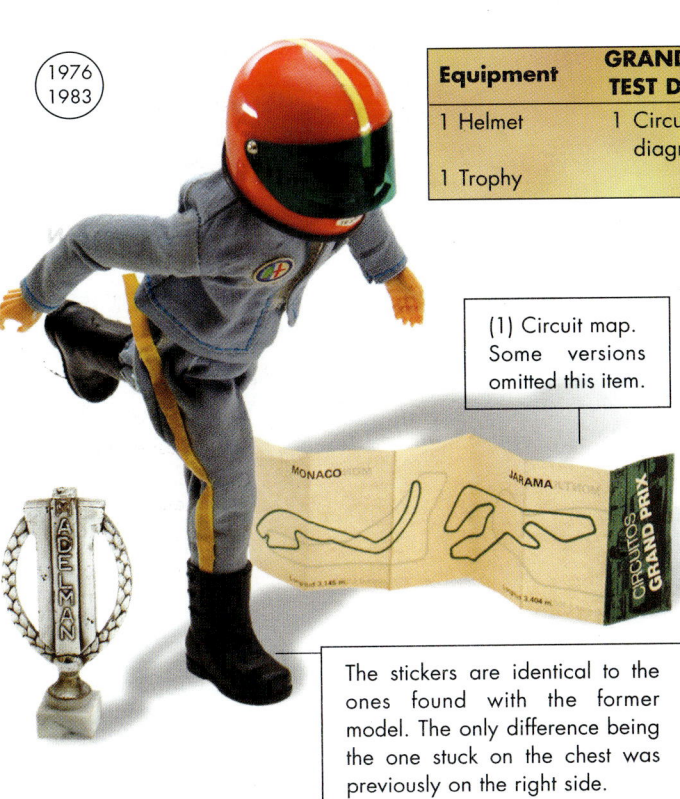

Equipment	GRAND PRIX TEST DRIVER
1 Helmet	1 Circuit diagram [1]
1 Trophy	

(1) Circuit map. Some versions omitted this item.

The stickers are identical to the ones found with the former model. The only difference being the one stuck on the chest was previously on the right side.

Equipment	GRAND PRIX MECHANIC & BOXES
1 Peaked cap	
1 Blackboard	
1 Box containing six tools	
1 Ferrari sticker on the chest with another on the back	

(1976 1983)

(1976 1983)

Equipment	HELICOPTER PILOT	
1 Peaked cap	1 Binoculars
1 Radio transmitter	1 Briefcase containing a map (battle lines)

(1976 1983)

Equipment	NAVY AIRCRAFT CARRIER SAILOR	
1 Helmet	2 Pennants
1 Binoculars	

A silver radio transmitter was included with the first version during the 'Second Stage'.

MADELMAN

1983

(1) Sailor's hat.
In both versions, the hat was not glued to the head.

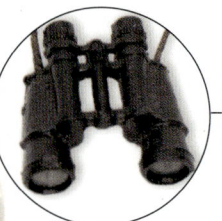

Detail of the binoculars supplied with both versions.

Equipment	NAVY MARINE
1 Helmet	
1 Pistol	
1 Radio transmitter	
1 Machine gun	

1976 1980

Equipment	NAVY SAILOR	
	1st Version	2nd Version
	1 Sailor's hat (1)	1 Sailor's hat
	1 Kitbag (without number)	1 Binoculars
	1 Binoculars	1 Red flashlight
	1 Red flashlight	1 Life vest

1976 1980

Equipment ARMY COMMANDO
1 Helmet
1 Radio transmitter
1 Machine gun

There is also an earlier version that included some hand grenades instead of the radio transmitter.

Equipment ARMY COMMUNICATIONS
1 Helmet
1 Green radio with earphones

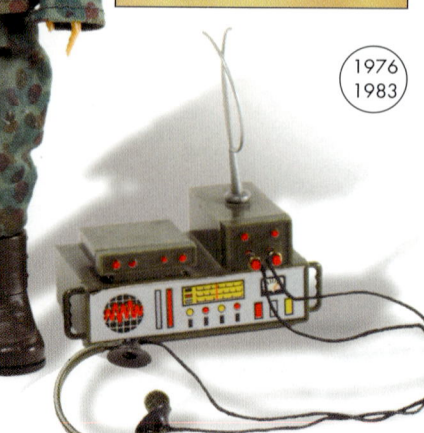

1976 1983

60

SECOND STAGE

1976
1983

Equipment	ARMY MILITARY POLICE
1 Helmet [1]	
1 Pistol	
1 Truncheon	
1 Radio transmitter	

(1) Helmet. The helmet shown here was an intermediate model. The first model was larger while the second was equipped with a rubber chinstrap fixed to the inside of the helmet.

1976
1977

Equipment	ARMY MEDIC
1 Helmet [1]	
1 Bag containing four medicine containers	

(1) Helmet. This set was only marketed during 1976. It came supplied with the 'First Stage' helmet such as the one seen here that is smaller and in a lighter shade.

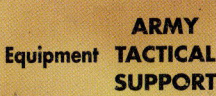

Equipment	ARMY TACTICAL SUPPORT
1 Helmet	
1 Bazooka	
2 Projectiles	

1976
1977

Equipment	ARMY ASSAULT TROOPER
1 Helmet [1]	
1 Machine gun	
1 Sandbag	

(1) Helmet. This model was only marketed during 1976 and 1977 and it retained the 'First Stage' helmet.

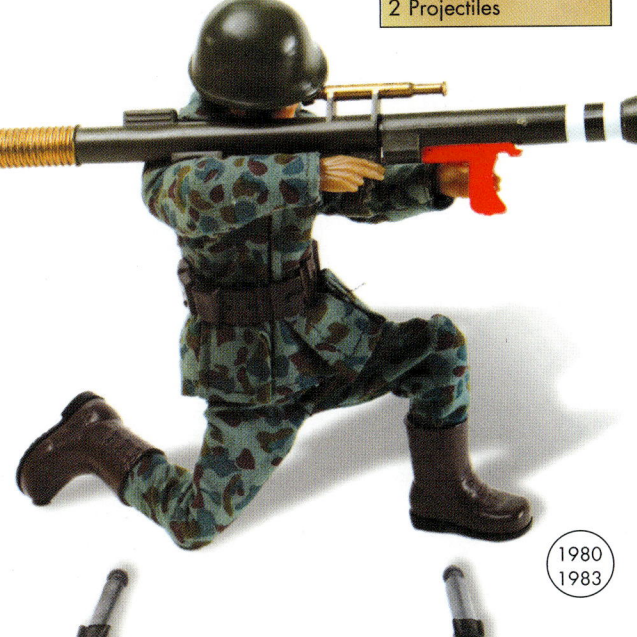

1980
1983

MADELMAN

Equipment	SPECIAL OPS
1 Peaked cap	1 Pistol [1]
1 Machine gun	1 Hook
1 Radio transmitter	

(1977 / 1983)

[1] Pistol. Neither holster not belt were available.

Detail of the hook released in two versions with this dummy.

Shown here are the two variants of the suit made by MADEL. The differences were in the colour and textures, one being made of plastic and the other of rubber.

Equipment	
WOODEN LEGGED PIRATE	
1 Rat	
1 Bucket	
1 Flintlock pistol	

(1976 / 1977)

Equipment	
PIRATES - BLACK JIM	
1 Spyglass	
1 Rum cask	
1 Cutlass	

(1976 / 1977)

SECOND STAGE

Equipment	FAR WEST WITCH DOCTOR
1 Amulet [1]	
1 Mask	
1 Shield	

1977
1983

Equipment	FAR WEST COW-BOY
1 Rubber hat	
1 Banjo	
1 Silver Colt	
1 Rope	

1977
1983

(1) Amulet. Four transverse bones, one vertical and with a skull on the upper part.

Equipment	FAR WEST - CARAVAN GUIDE	
1 Hat		1 Banjo
1 Winchester rifle		

1981
1983

The overalls for this dummy were somewhat darker that the ones supplied with the man from the 'Settler Couple' set.

Equipment	FAR WEST RUSTLER
1 Hat	
1 Saddlebags	
2 Gold bars	
1 Silver Colt	

1977
1983

63

MADELMAN

1977 / 1983

Equipment	FAR WEST SERGEANT, 7TH CAVALRY
1 Cap	1 Winchester rifle
1 Saddlebags	1 Map [1]
1 Silver Colt	

(1) Map.
Showed locations of North American Indian tribe settlements.

Equipment	FAR WEST INDIAN SCOUT
1 Hat	1 Silver Colt
1 Axe	1 Snake
1 Knife	

1977 / 1983

This set was introduced in the 1976 catalogue. It was to contain saddlebags as in the 'Hunter' set, although no sets containing this item were ever released.

1981 / 1983

Equipment	FAR WEST CAPTAIN, 7TH CAVALRY
1 Peaked cap	1 Binoculars
1 Silver Colt	1 Sabre [1]

(1) Sabre.
This was an exclusive item and was more stylized than the sword supplied with the 'Pirates' sets.

SECOND STAGE

Equipment	FAR WEST PINK FEATHER
1 Saucepan	1 Hair ribbon with a feather [1]
1 Baby harness	
1 Necklace	

1977 1980

Detail of the harness and the baby.

(1) Hair ribbon with a feather. The material used for this item was so fragile that it is impossible to find one in good condition.

1982 1983

Equipment	FAR WEST BLACK MOOSE
1 Pipe	1 Totem pole
1 Fur [1]	

(1) Fur.
Like the one supplied with the Sleigh' set but somewhat darker.

65

MADELMAN

Equipment	MADELMAN COSMIC SPACESHIP COMMANDER
1 Helmet	1 Knapsack

1980
1983

Equipment	MADELMAN COSMIC SPACE RESEARCHER
1 Helmet	1 Knapsack

1980
1983

Equipment	MADELMAN COSMIC SPACESHIP PILOT
1 Helmet	1 Gun (1)
1 Flashlight	

1980
1983

(1) Gun.
This was identical to the one supplied with the flamethrower set and was injection molded in translucent yellow plastic.

SECOND STAGE

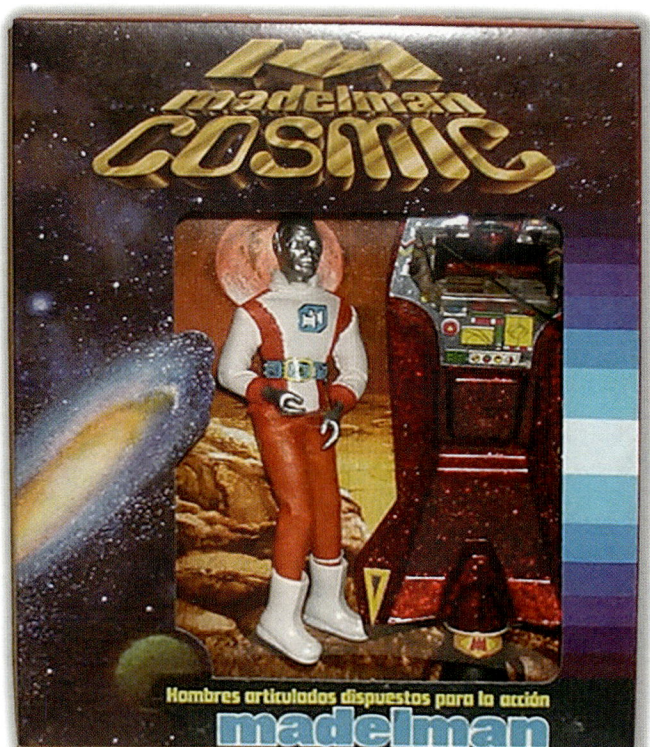

Equipment	MADELMAN COSMIC SPACE PATROL	1983
1 Scooter		

Please note that this figure is purposely displayed in its box because, like other clothes in the collection (Scuba Diver, Hunter, Mounted Police...), they are extremely fragile and handling of any kind must be avoided.

1980 / 1983

Equipment	MADELMAN COSMIC COSMIC LINKAGE
1 Helmet	1 Knapsack

1983

Equipment	MADELMAN COSMIC GREEN MAN
1 Helmet	1 Gun [1]
1 Knapsack	

(1) Gun.
This item possessed the identical frame as the 'Scuba Diver's' harpoon but was injection molded in glitter red.

MADELMAN

FOOTBALLERS

(1983)

The only accessories supplied with these sets were stickers with the player's number. From left to the right: England, Argentina, France, Brazil, Italy, Germany and Spain.

(1983)

This item has been displayed in its box as it is a very rare example of the original set and the mask has often been forged.

Equipment	MASKED MAN
1 Hat	1 Flintlock pistol
1 Sabre	

(1983)

Equipment	RED ARCHER
1 Hat	
1 Carcaj	
4 Arrows	
1 Bow	

SECOND STAGE

Basic equipment

Shown here are the Basic Equipment' sets that, as with the ones from the 'First Stage', contained a dummy plus more equipment than in the individual version.

Equipment	SAFARI GUIDE
1 Hat	1 Kenya safari map
1 Rifle	1 Panther
1 Silver Colt	1 Net
1 Water canteen	1 Machete

1977
1983

MADELMAN

Equipment	SHERIFF
1 Hat [1]	2 Pasquinades
1 Weapons shelf	3 Gold bars
2 Winchester rifle	1 Handcuffs
1 White sack [2]	2 Silver Colts
1 Water canteen	

1976
1983

(1) Hat.
The first version, as shown here, was made from felt, the second from rubber.

(2) White sack
with the word 'Post' on it.

70

SECOND STAGE

Equipment	GOLD PROSPECTOR
1 Hat	1 Spade
1 Banjo	1 Winchester rifle
1 Whiskey barrel	1 Water canteen
2 Small sacks	2 Dynamite charges
1 Wheelbarrow	1 Sieve

Shown here are the two different released versions. The first had the same face as 'Dick the One-Eyed' while the second had the identical face as the 'Spaceship Pilot' and the 'Rustler'.

1976
1983

MADELMAN

Equipment	INDIAN CHIEF
1 Shield	1 Carpet (map)
1 Spear	1 Winchester rifle
1 Totem pole	1 Plume
1 Peace pipe	

1976 1983

Shown here are the two different models released. The sole difference was the plume colour, the first was red and the second white with a different coloured tip.

SECOND STAGE

Equipment	INDIAN WARRIOR
1 Bow	
1 Quiver	
1 Arrows	
1 Tomahawk	
1 Winchester rifle	
1 Tom-tom	
1 Mask	
1 Snake	
1 Knife	
3 Crayons [1]	

 1976 1983

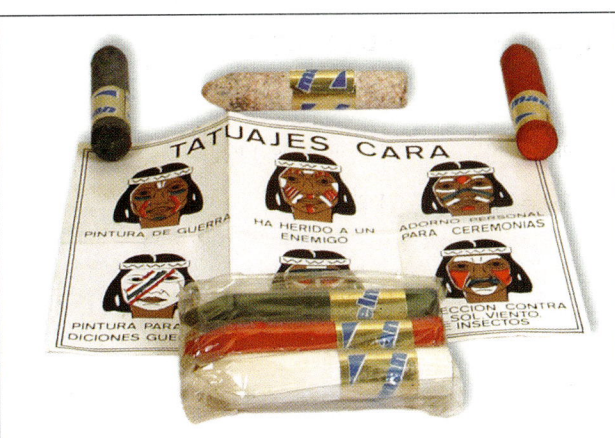

(1) Crayons. Used for applying war paint. Instructions were included.

This model was released in two different variants, the sole difference being the head.

MADELMAN

Equipment	DIVER
1 Diving suit	1 Rubber tube
1 Chest [1]	1 Air pump
1 Signal buoy	1 Knife and scabbard
1 Scapular	1 Pair of clogs [2]
1 Axe	

(1976 / 1983)

(1) Chest.
This contained a template for simulating gold coins.
The jewels were not manufactured during the 'First Stage'.

(2) Pair of clogs.
These were identical to those supplied with the 'First Stage' but adapted to the new boot.

(1) Operable trap.
The plastic used for the rifle, sleigh and trap was darker than that used during the 'First Stage'.

Equipment	HUNTER
1 Rubber hat	1 Rustic sleigh
1 Powder horn	1 Fox
1 Haversack	1 Chest
1 Knife	1 Operable trap [1]
1 Rifle	

(1976 / 1983)

SECOND STAGE

(1976 1983)

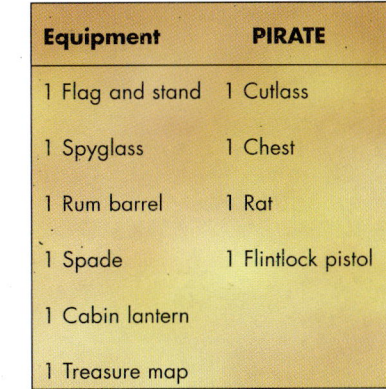

Equipment	PIRATE
1 Flag and stand	1 Cutlass
1 Spyglass	1 Chest
1 Rum barrel	1 Rat
1 Spade	1 Flintlock pistol
1 Cabin lantern	
1 Treasure map	

Spyglass detail.

Equipment PRIVATEER
1 Bicorn
1 Parrot
1 Powder keg
1 Spyglass
1 Cutlass
1 Box containing six musket balls
1 Cannon
1 Tamper
1 Flintlock pistol

(1976 1983)

MADELMAN

Equipment	SCUBA DIVER
1 Rubber raft and paddle	1 Watch
1 Cylinder	1 Flashlight
1 Goggles	1 Knife and scabbard
1 Harpoon	2 Dynamite charges

(1976 1983)

Equipment	POLAR EXPLORER
1 Whip	1 Dog and harness
1 Sleigh	1 Cooker
1 Blanket	2 Snowshoes

(1976 1983)

SECOND STAGE

Detail of the oxygen cylinders.

Equipment	COMMANDO
1 Hat	1 Hook and rope
6 Hand grenades	1 Detonator
3 Dynamite charges	1 Binoculars
1 Operable mortar	1 Pistol
1 Reel	1 Radio transmitter

1976 1983

MADELMAN

Equipment	ANTI-TANK	
1 Helmet	1 Flamethrower	1 Box with 3 projectiles
1 Pistol	1 Bazooka	6 Grenades

Equipment	INDIAN PRINCESS
1 Bonfire	1 Spyglass
1 Frame [(1)]	1 Plastic bale
1 Saucepan	1 Fishing net
1 Dog and sleigh	

(1) Frame. Two vertical and one horizontal poles plus a hook.

(2) Saucepan. This was suspended from the hook.

1977 1983

1976 1983

80

SECOND STAGE

(1977 / 1983)

Equipment	NURSE
1 Helmet with a red cross on it	1 Transparent bag with rubber bandages
1 Stretcher	1 Cotton roll
1 Transfusion equipment	1 White bottle
1 Dressing gown	1 Transparent bottle
1 Mask	1 Box with a red cross on the lid
1 Bag and stethoscope	

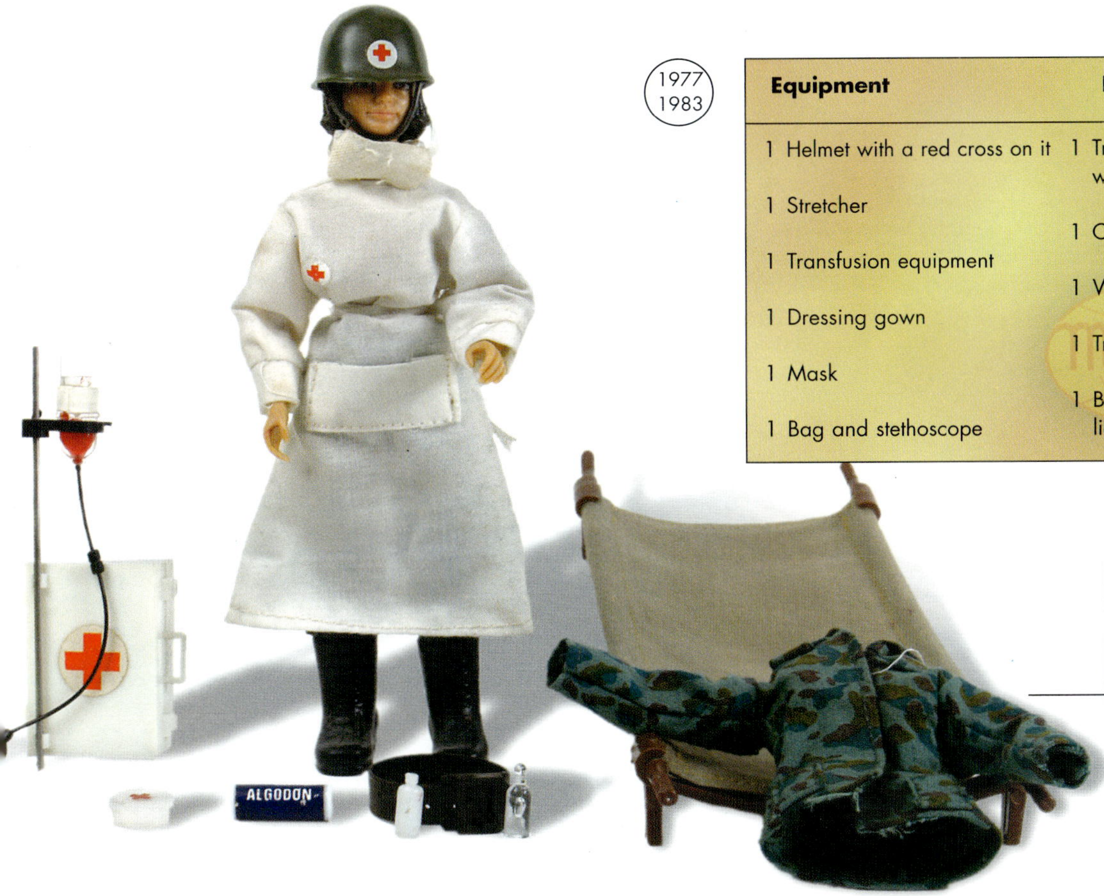

Seen here is the jacket that clearly shows the different cut to make it fit the doll's narrower waist.

(1976 / 1983)

Equipment	EXPLORER
1 Rubber hat	1 Machete
1 Chair	1 Rifle
1 Gas lantern (orange)	1 Snake
1 Radio transmitter	1 Chimpanzee
1 Silver Colt	1 Water canteen

MADELMAN

Equipment	PRIVATEER
1 Parrot	
1 Stand simulating bamboo on stony ground	
3 Rats	
1 Flintlock pistol	
1 Treasure map	
1 Cutlass	
1 Flag and stand	
1 Cabin lantern	
1 Bag containing jewels	

1977
1983

Super equipment

This section shows the 'Super Equipment' sets that, as with the earlier ones released during the First Stage, included two dummies and a large number of accessories.

Equipment	SUBMARINE RESEARCH (SCUBA DIVER AND DIVER)	
1 Anti-shark cag	1 Signal buoy	2 Clogs
1 Goggles	1 Air pump	1 Axe
1 Oxygen cylinders	1 Tube (1)	1 Chest containing jewels
1 Harpoon	1 Yellow diving suit	
1 Flashlight	1 Seahorse	2 Stars (2)
1 Shark	1 Scapular	2 Knives with scabbards

Here can be seen the variations in colour and texture between the first version (right) and the second one (left).

SECOND STAGE

(1) Tube.
The difference with the other scuba divers is that the tube is orange.

(2) Stars.
One large and one smal.

1980
1983

MADELMAN

REDSKINS
INDIAN WARRIOR AND PINK FEATHER

Equipment			
1 Map [1]	1 Spear	1 Quiver containing four arrows	1 Sleigh
1 Winchester rifle	1 Knife	1 Snake	1 Bonfire and sticks [3]
1 Bow	1 Pipe	1 Dappled horse [2]	1 Fishing net
1 Tomahawk	1 Shield		

1977 / 1980

(2) Dappled horse.
The difference between this horse and the one that was sold on its own was that the former was not equipped with blanket, bridle or reins.

(3) Bonfire and sticks.
This item did not include the saucepan or hook like the one supplied with the Indian Princess set.

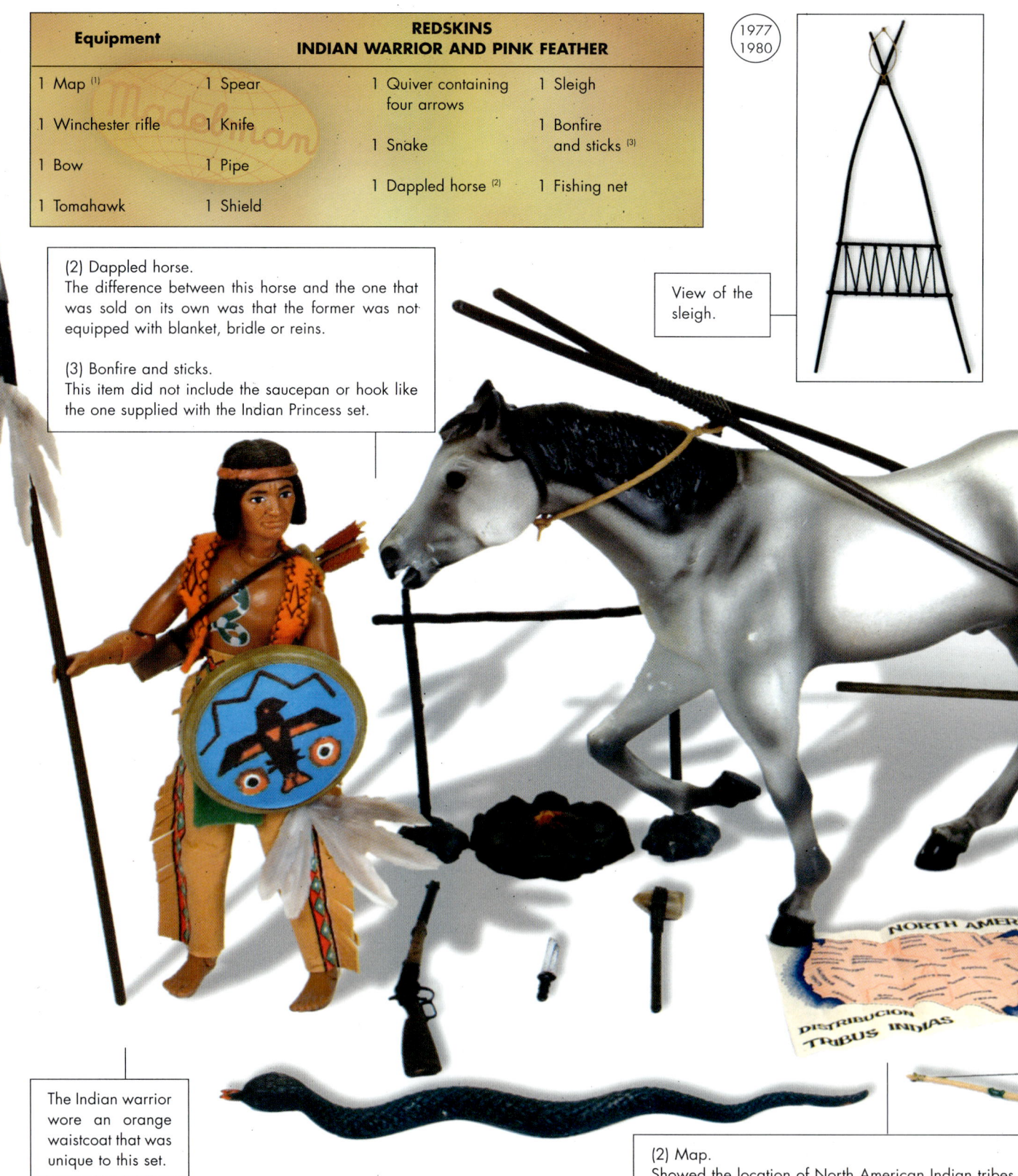

View of the sleigh.

The Indian warrior wore an orange waistcoat that was unique to this set.

(2) Map.
Showed the location of North American Indian tribes.

SECOND STAGE

1977 / 1980

Equipment	SETTLERS
1 Coffee pot	1 Cup
1 Saucepan	1 Bonfire
1 Frying pan	1 Grill
1 Dish	

This set was different from the others in the 'Super Equipment' series. It contained fewer accessories, although it did include two figures.

The settlers' hats were released in two different colours.

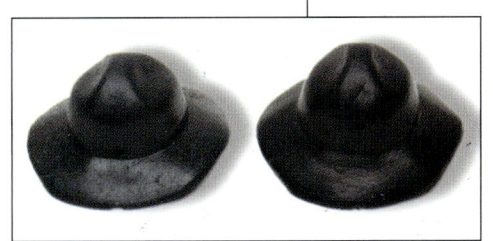

MADELMAN

Equipment	PIRATE CAPTAIN ONE-EYED DICK AND WOODEN LEG	
1 Raft [1]	1 Bucket	1 Ball and chain
1 Cabin lantern	1 Rum cask	1 Bottle of rum
1 Treasure map	1 Dynamite keg	1 Spyglass
1 Oar	1 Spade	
1 Boathook	1 Flintlock pistol	

Although this item was not included in the catalogues during the Second Stage, it is known that this version contained old dummies in old packaging. The raft was made in a darker plastic than the original one. It was only sold during 1976.

1976 / 1977

(1) Raft.
Containing stand for the parrot and a flag pole.

SECOND STAGE

1982 / 1983

Equipment	CANADA MOUNTED POLICE AND HUNTER	
1 Bale	1 Radio transmitter	1 Dog
1 Winchester rifle	1 Rustic sleigh	1 White snowshoes
1 Rifle	1 Bonfire	1 Sorrel horse
1 Barrel	1 Operable trap	1 Canoe and two paddles

MADELMAN

This Madelman was commonly known as 'White Skier'.

SECOND STAGE

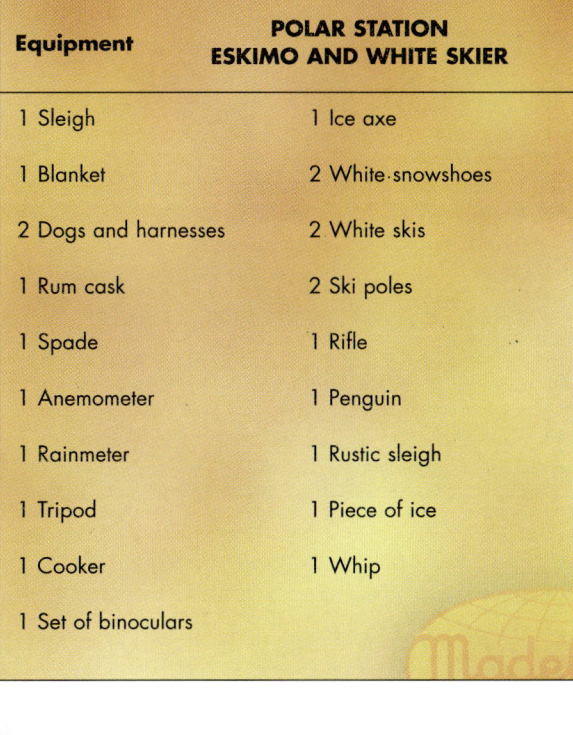

1982
1983

Equipment	POLAR STATION ESKIMO AND WHITE SKIER	
1 Sleigh	1 Ice axe
1 Blanket	2 White snowshoes
2 Dogs and harnesses	2 White skis
1 Rum cask	2 Ski poles
1 Spade	1 Rifle
1 Anemometer	1 Penguin
1 Rainmeter	1 Rustic sleigh
1 Tripod	1 Piece of ice
1 Cooker	1 Whip
1 Set of binoculars	

Detail of the penguin.

MADELMAN

Equipment	KENYA SAFARI HUNTER AND PORTER
1 Lion (1)	1 Binoculars
1 Tent	1 Rifle
1 Table	1 Silver Colts
2 Chairs	1 Radio and earphones
1 Blue gas lamp	1 Eight-sided cage
2 Monkeys	1 Kenya safari map
1 White cloth bag containing four medicine containers	4 Elephant tusks

1976 1980

(1) Lion.
In some sets, this was replaced by a panther.

(2) Radio and earphones.
In this 'Super Equipment' set the radio had a white front panel with a brown one on the back.

This was the first version marketed from 1976 – 1980.

SECOND STAGE

This was the second version released in 1980.

1980
1983

Equipment	KENYA GUIDE AND PORTER
1 Tent	1 Table
2 Plastic bales	1 Rifle
2 Monkeys	1 Water canteen
1 Barrel	1 Bonfire
1 Net	2 Elephant tusks
1 Lion	
2 Silver Colts	

Detail of the lion.

MADELMAN

Equipment	HIGH COMMAND OFFICER AND ASSAULT TROOP SOLDIER	1976 1983
1 Tent	1 Briefcase with map (2)	
1 Bazooka	1 Mortar	
2 Ammunition boxes (1)	1 Radio and earphones	
1 Machine gun	1 Blue gas lamp	
1 Table	6 Hand grenades	
1 Chair		

(1) Ammunition box.
Each box contained five projectiles for the bazooka.

(2) Briefcase and map.
High command attack

There was also a later version that included a flamethrower and a green jerry can. A sandbag was deleted and more mortar ammunition was added.

SECOND STAGE

Complements

Shown here are the accessories that, in this Second Stage, also included the scooter, the green helicopter, cannon and motorboat. New references were added later.

Equipment	CARAVAN WAGON
1 Large barrel	1 Pick
3 Plastic bales	1 Spade
1 Bucket	1 Whip

1977
1983

This wagon had an optional handbrake, an operable tailgate, and a box fixed to the chassis. It also had a wheel that fixed to the central shaft between the horses that, together with the wagon's wheels, allowed it to be moved.

MADELMAN

CANNON

1976
1983

This item was sold without accessories, just as shown here. However, sometimes, a couple of ammunition boxes were included.

Equipment	FORTIFIED POSITION 2 ASSAULT TROOPS MADELMAN
6 Poles and 1 net	2 Machine guns
2 Ammunition boxes for the cannon	1 Cannon

1977
1980

This item had a working door.

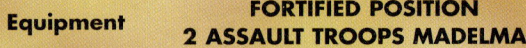

SECOND STAGE

Equipment	JEEP TRAILER
1 Spare wheel	1 Green jerry can

1973
1975

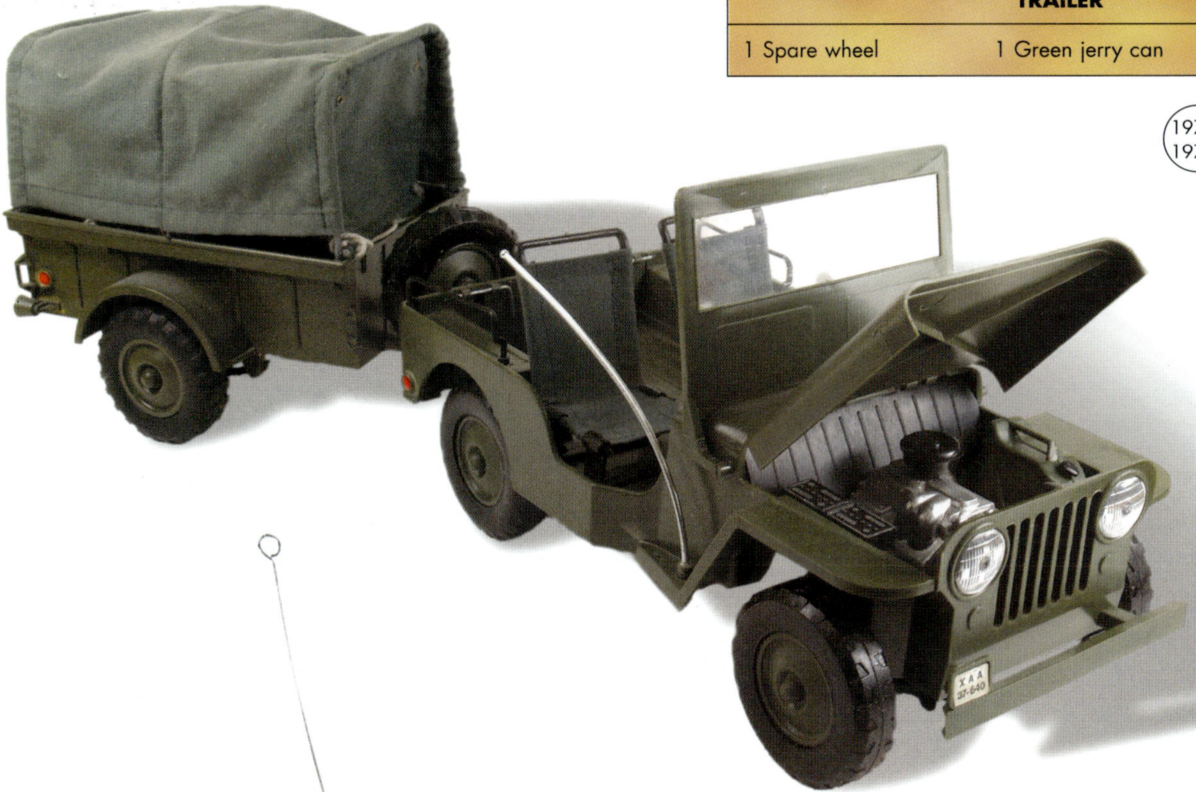

BUGGY EXPLORER

1978
1983

The first buggies released were manufactured by the Froba company. Madelman later purchased the company and began producing their own models.

One of the models made by Froba.

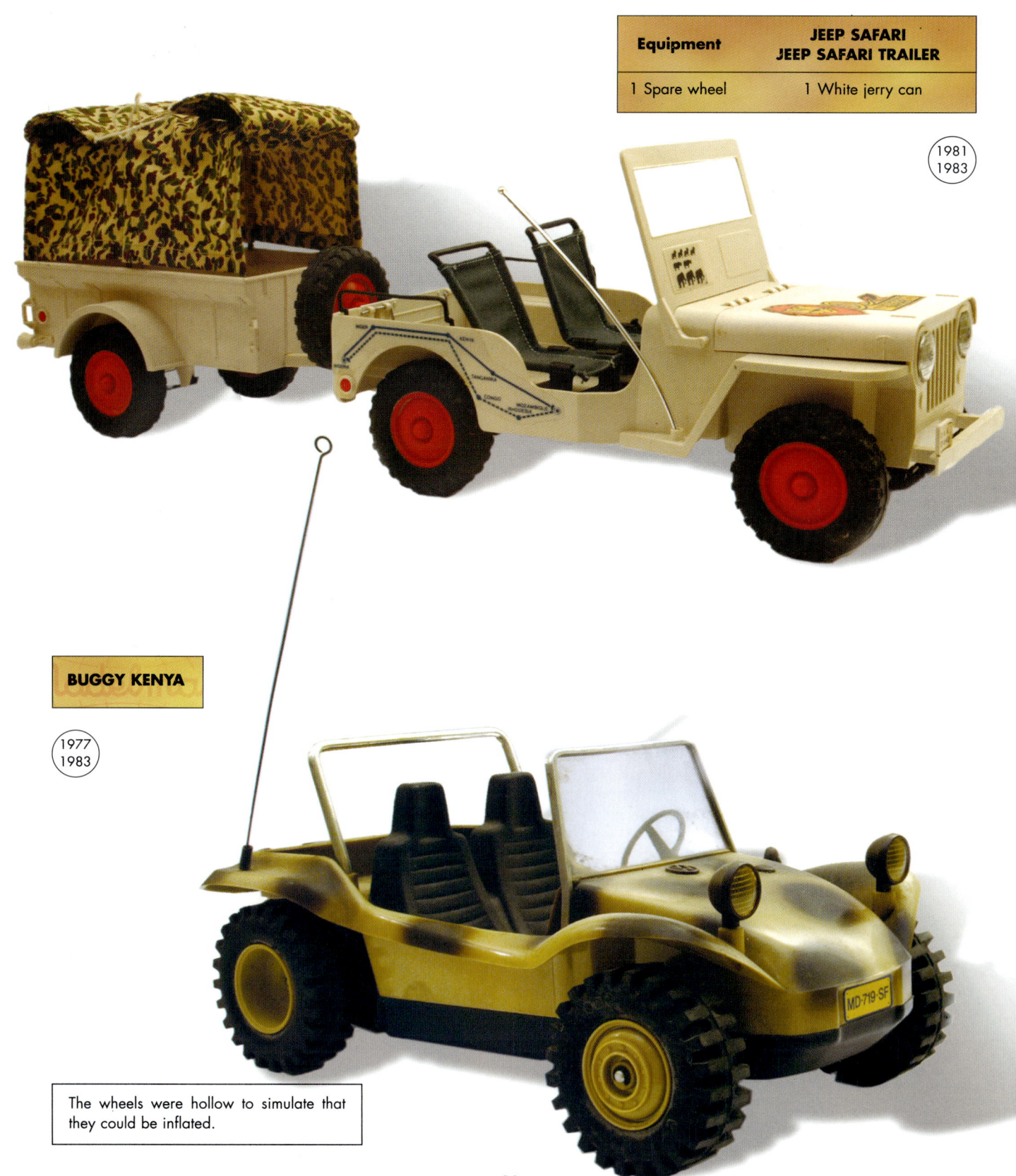

SECOND STAGE

SLEIGH (1976/1980)

The differences compared to the previous model was that the new one was injection molded in darker plastic and the dog, which could be also found in the Indian Princess Equipment.

Equipment LAUNCH

1 Oar

1 Anchor

(1976/1980)

SCOOTER

(1976/1980)

This is one of the few items never redesigned by Madel. It remained the same throughout its life.

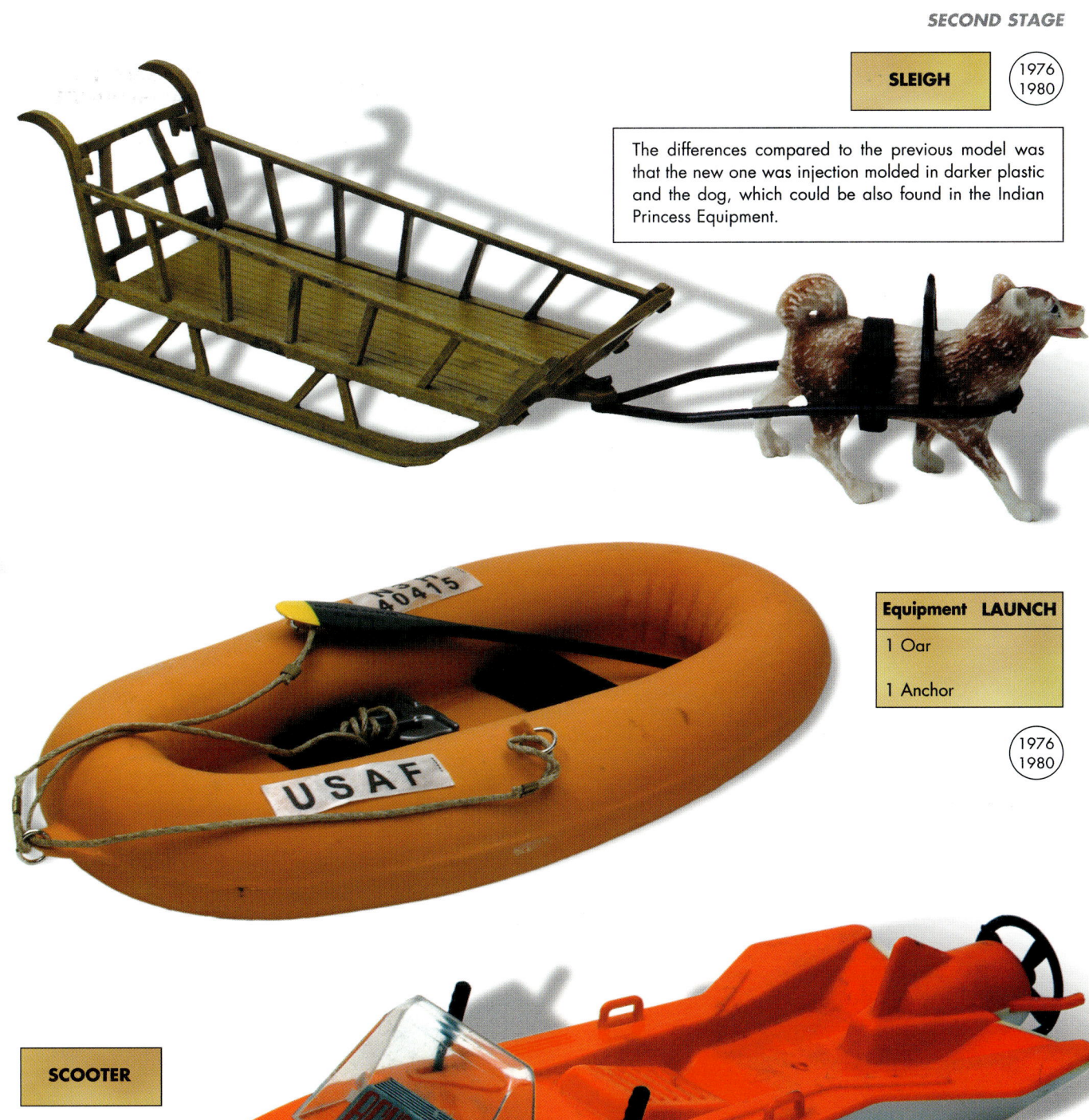

MADELMAN

RESCUE HELICOPTER

1977
1983

This item was equipped with a stretcher and two green slings that could be fixed to a working hook.

HELICOPTER

1975
1983

The helicopters were undoubtedly the most popular items made by Madel. They even achieved international recognition with an honorific mention in Stitching Goed Speel Goed European 1976.

SECOND STAGE

HELICOPTER MISSILE-LAUNCHING

1977
1983

This helicopter was fitted with six rocket launch tubes and these could be fired via a spring-loaded system.

HELICOPTER SUPERMAN

1978
1983

This is probably the only truly ridiculous Madel release as, obviously, Superman doesn't require a helicopter to fly!

MADELMAN

SUPERMAN

1978
1983

This dummy was released in 1978 (the same year that the movie was first released in Spain) and it had the torso of a male Madelman and the legs of a female. There were two versions of the boots in the picture.

BUGGY SUPERMAN

1978
1980

This vehicle was made from Tilsen Polystyrene, a plastic with metallic powder added.

SECOND STAGE

Equipment	TEPEE
1 Totem pole	
1 Frame [1]	
1 Saucepan	
1 Bonfire	

1977
1983

(1) Two vertical and one horizontal poles plus a hook.

Equipment	KAYAK
1 Bale	2 Paddles

1977
1983

103

MADELMAN

DAPPLE HORSE

1977
1983

Both horses were released in 1977. The bodies were made from polystyrene and the saddles and bridles from PVC.

1977
1983

SORREL HORSE

MACHINE GUN 7ᵀᴴ CAVALRY

1981
1983

This piece was supplied with two magazines each containing eight rounds and was exclusive to this set. It was an operable machine gun, like the mortar and cannon.

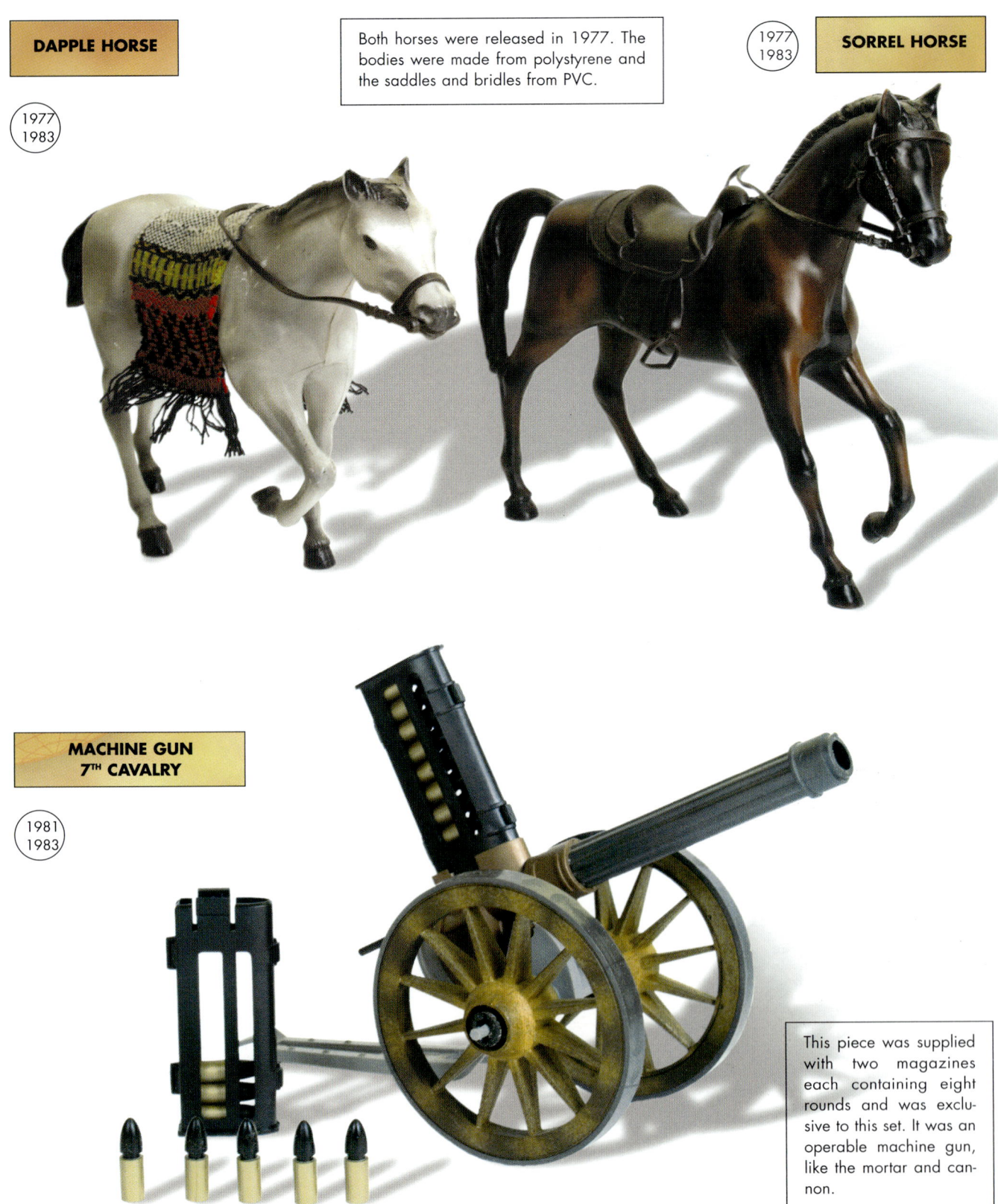

104

SECOND STAGE

SPACESHIP M7X

(1980 / 1983)

This is the first of the spaceships to be released and it is undoubtedly one of the best designs ever made both aesthetically and functionally.

SPACESHIP M7X INTERCOM

(1982 / 1983)

This craft was equipped with a walkie-talkie system (one inside the spaceship and another outside). It also had a battery compartment for powering the lights. A more sought-after version was powered by a dynamo.

The rear was left open so that a child could look inside and feel as though he was an actual spaceship pilot.

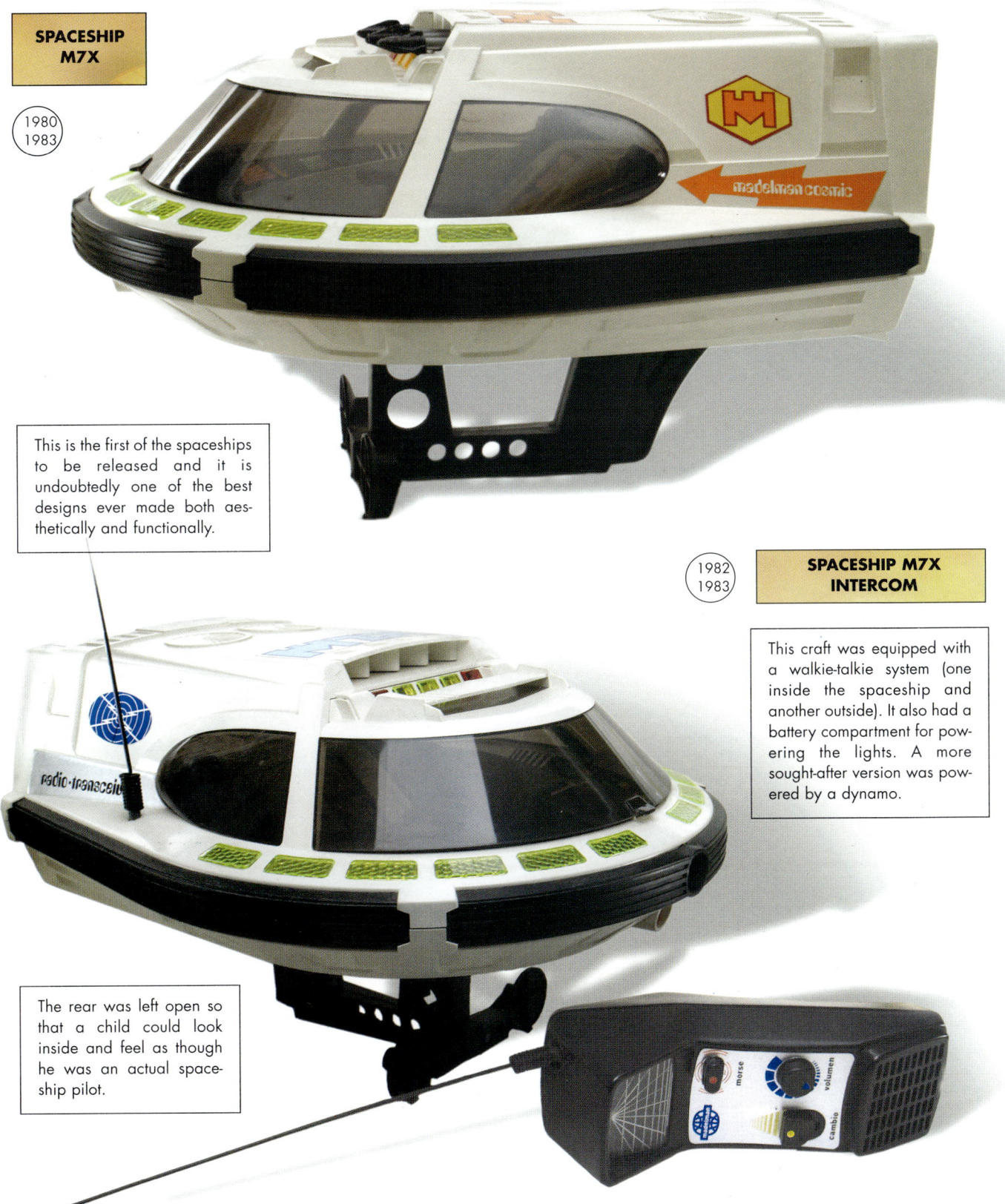

MADELMAN

SPECIAL SETS

These are the contents of the six 'Special Sets' released by MADEL. They all contain items already shown earlier in the book. However, the mine detector and the two mines should be highlighted as they were unique to this series.

Detail of the two mines and the detector.

Equipment	WEST 1	1977 1980
2 Handcuffs		
1 Sheriff's hat	1 Chest [3]	
1 Holster rig [1]	1 Sabre and flag	
1 Weapons shelf	1 Knife	
1 Winchester rifle	1 Sieve	
2 Pasquinades [2]	1 Spade	
1 Banjo	1 Wheelbarrow	
1 Gold prospector's hat	1 Cooker	

(1) Holster rig.
With two guns.

(2) Pasquinades.
For the Sheriff.

(3) Chest.
With a template to simulate gold coins.

Equipment	PIRATE	1977 1980
1 Spyglass	1 Raft (with mast and paddle)	
1 Flintlock pistol	1 Rum cask	
1 Knife	1 Parrot	
1 Belt	1 Boathook	
1 Bicorn hat	1 Sabre and flag	

The 'West 1' set contained the 'Sheriff' and the 'Gold Prospector' accessories, although items, such as the chest and the heather, were exclusive to this set.

The raft in the 'Pirate' set was injection molded in a darker plastic than the one included in the 'Pirate Super Equipment'.

Equipment	WEST 2	1977/1980
1 Tom-tom	1 Quiver with arrows	
1 Snake	1 Bow	
1 Map [1]	1 Plume [2]	
1 Spear	1 Peace pipe	
1 Totem pole	1 Shield [3]	
1 Tomahawk		

(1) Map.
Indian Chief.

(2) Plume.
Second version of the Indian Chief.

(3) Shield.
Black eagle on a blue background.

Equipment	ARMY	1977/1980
1 Mortar	1 Mine detector	
1 Ammunition box [1]	1 Hook	
1 Plan [2]	1 Detonator	
1 Helmet	1 Reel and stand [4]	
1 Peaked cap [3]	1 Radio transmitter	
1 Machine gun		
3 Dynamite charges		

(1) Ammunition box.
Containing rounds for the mortar.

(2) Plan.
Battle lines.

(3) Peaked cap.
Climber and sapper.

(4) Reel and stand.
Commando.

As can be seen in the 'West 2' description, it contained items from the 'Indian Chief' and 'Warrior' sets. The concept of putting together small accessories that were already included in other sets was a deliberate decision.
It should be underlined that the 'Scuba Diver' set contained the octopus from the 'Submarine Research' set from the First Stage.
The 'Army' set contained a unique design of the mine and detector.
The 'Polar' set included an ice axe, barrel and a rustic sleigh that had respectively been included in the 'Mountain Troop', 'Pirates' and 'Canada' sets.

Equipment	SUBMARINES	1977/1980
2 Rubber flippers	1 Goggles	
2 Stars [1]	1 Oxygen cylinders	
1 Harpoon [2]	1 Axe	
1 Knife	1 Submarine scooter	
1 Tube	1 Signal buoy	
1 Belt and weights	1 Seahorse	
1 Watch		

(1) Stars.
Large and small.

(2) Harpoon.
Made of plastic.

Equipment	POLAR	1977/1980
1 Anemometer	1 Spade	
1 Rainmeter	2 White snowshoes	
1 Tripod	1 Ice axe	
1 Cooker	1 Black binoculars	
1 Rifle with telescopic sight	1 Piece of ice	
1 Rustic sleigh	1 Penguin	
1 Rum cask		

EPILOGUE

After Madel closed its doors in 1982, many sets continued to be discovered in shops for some considerable time. However, once the collecting fever hit, they soon disappeared. It was not until after the advent of the new millennium that new initiatives, such as those by the likes of Altaya and Popular de Juguetes, saw the re-release of Madelman. Through these initiatives, many enthusiasts met their old childhood friends once again and while others discovered these wonderful dummies for first time.

One of the dummies released by Altaya and made by Popular de Juguetes. Right – one of the new Madelman.

A diorama constructed using dummies and accessories from the First and Second Madelman series.

INDEX

Prologue 3
Introduction 4

FIRST STAGE

Red boxes
Sailor 6
Assault troops 6
Mountain troops 6
Astronaut 2001 7
Safari hunter 7
Porter 7

Singles
Mountain troops – Climber 10
Safari hunter 10
Porter 10
Mountain troop – Sapper 11
Polar expedition – Snowshoes 11
Speleologist 11
Polar expedition – Skis 11
Polar expedition – Troop 12
Scuba diver – Reconnaissance 12
Scuba diver – Demolition 12
Navy – Sailor 13
Navy – Marine 13
Navy – Aircraft carrier service 13
Army – Communications 14
Army – Military police 14
Army – Commando 14
Army – Medic 15
Army – Assault troops 15
Grand Prix – Boxes mechanic 16
Grand Prix – Test pilot 16
Space research – Astronaut 2001 17
Canada – Mounted Police 17
Canada – Hunter 17
Pirates – Jim Black 18
Air Force – Helicopter pilot 18
Pirates – Wooden Leg 18

Basic Equipment Sets
Mountain troop 19
Scuba diver 20
Service station mechanic 20
Army – Medic 21
Speleologist 22
Polar expedition 22
Hunter 23
Canadian Mounted Police 26
Diver 27
Antitank 28
Safari guide 28
Commando 29
Pirate 30

Super Equipment
Kenya safari 30

Polar station 32
High command 33
Submarine research 34
Pirate captain 35

Complements
Green helicopter 37
Cannon 37
Jeep Safari 38
Trailer Safari 38
Jeep 38
Scooter 39
Launch 39
Sleigh 39

Accessories
Accessories 40

Missions
Safari mission 42
Camping mission 44

Catalogues and posters
Catalogues 46
Posters 47

Boxes
First stage 48
Second stage 50

SECOND STAGE

Individuals
Safari – Hunter 52
Safari – Scout 52
Safari – Porter 52
Speleology – Speleologist 53
Polar expedition – Skis 53
Polar expedition – Snowshoes 53
Mountain Troop – Sapper 54
Polar Expedition – Meteorologist 54
Polar Expedition – Troop 54
Mountain Troop – Climber 55
Scuba Diver – Reconnaissance 55
Scuba Diver – Demolition 55
Canada – Hunter 58
Canada – Mounted Police 58
Pirates – Dick the One-eyed 58
Space Research – Astronaut 2001 58
Grand Prix – Test pilot 59
Grand Prix – Boxes mechanic 59
Air Force – Helicopter pilot 59
Navy – Aircraft carrier sailor 59
Navy – Marine 60
Navy – Sailor 60
Army – Commando 60
Army – Communications 60
Army – Military Police 61

INDEX

Army – Medic 61
Army – Assault troops 61
Army – Tactical support 61
Special ops 62
Pirates – Wooden Leg 62
Pirates – Jim Black .62
Far West – Witch doctor 63
Far West – Cowboy 63
Far West – Caravan guide 63
Far West – Rustler .63
Far West – 7th cavalry sergeant 64
Far West – Indian explorer 64
Far West – 7th cavalry captain 64
Far West – Pink Plume 65
Far West – Black Moose 65
Madelman Cosmic – Spaceship commander 66
Madelman Cosmic – Space researcher 66
Madelman Cosmic – Spaceship pilot 66
Madelman Cosmic – Space patrol 67
Madelman Cosmic – Cosmic linkage 67
Madelman Cosmic – Green man 67
Footballers 68
Masked man 68
Red archer 68

Basic Equipment
Safari guide 69
Sheriff 70
Gold prospector 71
Indian chief 74
Indian warrior 75
Diver 76
Hunter 76
Pirate 77
Privateer 77
Polar explorer 78
Scuba diver 79
Commando 79
Anti-tank 80
Indian princess 80
Nurse 81
Explorer 81
Privateer (doll) 82

Super equipment
Submarine research 82
Redskins 84
Settlers 85
Pirate captain 86
Canada 87
Polar station 91
Kenya safari (1976) 92
Kenya safari (1980) 93
High command 94

Complements
Caravan wagon 95
Cannon 96
Fortified position .96
Jeep 97
Buggy explorer 97
Jeep safari 98
Buggy Kenya 98
Sleigh 99
Motorboat 99
Scooter 99
Rescue helicopter 100
Helicopter 100
Missile launcher helicopter 100
Helicopter Superman 101
Superman 102
Buggy Superman .102
Tepee 103
Kayak 103
Dappled horse 104
Sorrel horse 104
7th cavalry machine gun 104
Spaceship M7x 105
Spaceship M7x intercom 105

Special sets
Mine detector 106
Far West 1 106
Pirate 106
Far West 2 107
Army 107
Scuba diving 107
Polar 107

Epilogue 109

I would like to express my thanks to my friend, SEZAR BLUE, without whose invaluable assistance this book would never have come to fruition. Thanks also to PEDRO LOZANO whose pictures and documentation have been of immense help.

Pedro Andrea